Legacy of Grace

Michelle Pace

Legacy of Grace
Copyright © 2016 by Michelle Pace

All rights reserved. No part of this book may be reproduced or transmitted in any form or by any means without written permission from the author.

Unless otherwise noted Scripture quotations are from The Holy Bible, King James Version. Scripture quotations marked (NIV) are taken from the Holy Bible, New International Version®, NIV®. Copyright © 1973, 1978, 1984, 2011 by Biblica, Inc.™ Used by permission of Zondervan. All rights reserved worldwide. www.zondervan.com The "NIV" and "New International Version" are trademarks registered in the United States Patent and Trademark Office by Biblica, Inc.™ Scripture quotations marked (AMP) are taken from the Amplified Bible, Copyright © 1954, 1958, 1962, 1964, 1965, 1987 by The Lockman Foundation. Used by permission.

ISBN 978-0-578-18198-1

Printed in the United States of America

Dedication

To my three children, McKenzi, Ashton, and London, for being a light in our home and to this generation, for being faithful and steadfast, and for adding a dimension of love and joy to our lives that words cannot express.

To my four grandchildren, Nicollet, Jordin, Charlie, and Jillian, I pray you will always love the Lord and trust Him.

To my dear friends, Laurie and Donna, who had to endure reading this script several times as I made changes, for always prayerfully supporting me and being a source of constant strength and encouragement.

To sweet Sara Woods and my daughter McKenzi for spending much of their precious time to edit this work. The Lord knows I could not have done this without your help.

To Pastor David O. Walters for teaching me godly principles and being an example of living a committed life for Jesus Christ.

To my current pastor and pastor's wife, Bro Mike and Shirley Chuppe, for all the hours of Bible Study that brought me to the revelation of Jesus Christ and the plan of salvation.

Above all, to Jesus Christ for His abundant mercy and grace and for blessing me beyond measure! I can say with the Psalmist, "My cup runneth over."

4

Table of Contents

Foreword 7

Introduction 9

Chapter 1 11

Chapter 2 19

Chapter 3 23

Chapter 4 27

Chapter 5 31

Chapter 6 37

Chapter 7 41

Chapter 8 45

Chapter 9 53

Chapter 10 63

Chapter 11 67

Chapter 12 71

Chapter 13 75

Chapter 14 77

Chapter 15 81

Chapter 16 87

Chapter 17 91

Chapter 18 95

Chapter 19 99

Chapter 20 103

Chapter 21 111

Chapter 22 115

Chapter 23 121

Chapter 24 127

Chapter 25 137

Chapter 26 141

Chapter 27 145

Chapter 28 149

Chapter 29 151

Chapter 30 153

Chapter 31 155

Chapter 32 161

Chapter 33 165

Chapter 34 167

Chapter 35 169

Chapter 36 175

Contact the Author....................................... 177

Foreword

Are you fighting life's battles? Is there hurt, sickness, loneliness or emptiness in your life? If you answered yes to any of these questions, then Michelle Pace's *Legacy of Grace* will encourage you! *Legacy of Grace* is a true story, a testimony of God's longsuffering love, His miraculous mercy, and His great grace! This book is about a hurting wife seeking after God and a husband and father needing God but not knowing God or understanding God's grace.

As the author's pastor, I am honored to write this foreword. My wife and I, the teachers of Michelle's first Bible study, witnessed Michelle taking a stand for God when her friends thought there was too much required and when her husband was not interested in God either. There were many disappointments along the way and many emotional scars that God had to work on, but He is faithful, and He was able to bring Michelle through these many disappointments.

Legacy of Grace captures the formative years of Michelle's life and takes you through the struggles in her marriage and the growth of her family. Then comes a difficult time when her dad has cancer, and she agrees to have a Bible study. Her acceptance of God brought many changes to her social life and her. There were many trials and years of despair; later there was a miracle that got Todd's attention. As the book continues, the family enters into a time of health issues for Todd. You will see the grace of God at work in their lives.

You will find in this book that living for God does not exempt us from trials. As Job 23:10 says, "But he knoweth the way that I take: [when] he hath tried me, I shall come forth as gold." Yes, God has a way that I do not fully understand of taking our trials and turning us into gold.

Todd, Michelle, McKenzi, Ashton and London have experienced, tasted and enjoyed God's love, mercy, and grace! Now they possess the Legacy of Grace!

Pastor Michael M. Chuppe
The Sanctuary, Bismarck, ND

Introduction

The Lord nudged me over nine years ago during a ladies' convention to write a book. The impression that I was to write a book took me off guard; the thought of writing a book had never crossed my mind. I certainly was not thinking along those lines while I was intently listening to our conference speaker.

The still small voice I heard that day was so strong that I took the time to write it down in my journal. Truthfully, I quickly forgot about it, but evidently, the Lord did not. Over the last three years the Lord began to deal with me more specifically on writing my story. I do not consider myself an author. I have written this book out of obedience to the Lord's prompting.

The book is written about my own life experiences of being saved and facing opposition from within my own household. It tells of a promise made to me by the Lord.

This book will take you on a journey and show you how the Lord patiently and lovingly reaches for souls. Specifically, how the Lord saved me and has answered my prayers in His perfect will and timing. Before I even realized I needed more of God's Truth to have salvation, He was working out a plan in my life to bring me to the fulness of His Truth.

I pray that in some way, even if small, it touches the heart of the reader and brings encouragement to stay the course with Jesus. After all, He knows what is best. My hope is that the Lord somehow will use my story as a source of encouragement. May it bring hope to someone who has been hanging on in prayer and reassure them that God is working, even when your eyes can't see. He is faithful!

10

Chapter One
Looking Back

As I sat down to write this book, my mind traveled down memory lane, reflecting on God's AMAZING grace. I can see His grace weaving into my life over the last 25 years and His goodness and mercy tracing back into my childhood.

I was born into a traditional German Catholic home and was raised and reared in the traditions of Catholicism. My parents, dedicated and loyal to what they believed, did their best to train and instill the same belief system into my siblings and me. They worked hard and sacrificed financially to give us a private-school, Catholic education.

As a young child I had a great desire to learn all I could about our family religion. I memorized the required prayers needed to receive the sacraments of communion and entered the confessional to confess my sins to our parish priest. I clearly remember, at about the age of seven, taking our large family Bible to our kitchen table with the desire to read it from cover to cover. I was soon overwhelmed with the task, deciding I would try another time. My desires were right and sincere, but I needed someone to read the Bible with me and show me the way.

"How then shall they call on him in whom they have not believed? and how shall they believe in him of whom they have not heard? and how shall they hear without a preacher?"
(Romans 10:14)

As a student at a private Catholic school, church attendance was a daily part of my life during the school year. My family also attended on Sundays and every other required day of Holy obligation. I am thankful for the example of commitment, reverence, and respect for the house of God that my parents not only talked about but also lived before us. Even though we were not walking in the fulness of Truth, my parents instilled in me the basic principle of faithfulness to something you believe.

We as Apostolic parents must live out loud what we say we believe. We must endeavor to show our children that faithfulness matters if we want them to continue walking in Truth. Without Truth, all my parents could offer us was tradition. They could not lead us or aid us in developing the personal relationship with Jesus Christ that we all so desperately needed. We were empty vessels attempting to be Christians and failing miserably.

Over the next few years, my longing and curiosity for the things of God became dimmed by my own fleshly wants and desires. I worried more about spending time and having fun with my growing group of friends. We developed deviant behaviors as early as the age of ten. Sleepovers included playing what we thought were innocent séance games, listening to rock-n-roll music, and on occasion, sneaking liquor from our parents' liquor cabinets. I was only eleven years old the first time I experienced being drunk. We, of course, thought we were having fun and were just so cool. Little did I know how uncool I really was and how much farther these escapades were going to take me in a very short amount of time.

I have watched children grow up in seemingly wholesome and godly homes and get involved in some pretty crazy lifestyles. I questioned God on why and how this happens. One night, while thinking about my own life and how far I went astray, God impressed upon me that just coming from good homes, even Apostolic homes, is not enough. I felt like He answered, **"Empty vessels will be filled with something, either My Spirit or the lusts and spirits of this world."** We must be intentional about teaching our children God's Word and being a walking example of how to follow hard after Him, even in the midst of difficult times. We must strive to remain faithful and committed to the gospel, to put our trust and confidence in God, and to teach our children first of all, *"Hear, O Israel: The LORD our god is one LORD:" (Deuteronomy 6:4)* We also must purposefully instruct them whenever given the opportunity.

"And thou shalt teach them diligently unto thy children, and shalt talk of them when thou sittest in thine house, and when thou walkest by the way, and when thou liest down, and when thou risest up." (Deuteronomy 6:7)

My parents taught me how to go through the motions of being a "good" Catholic. We endanger our children's salvation if we merely show them how to adhere to Pentecostal traditions of dress and worship and never instill into them WHY we do what we do. We cannot make them love God and, yes, one day they will have to choose for themselves whom they will serve, but we must do everything possible to show them in God's Word why we believe what we do. Then, we must walk the walk and not just talk the talk. Kids are intuitive and can easily sense when someone is genuine. It saddens me when I see young people who have been in church all their lives and still not know simple truths from God's Word. Good kids can go bad! Good kids with no revelation and relationship with Jesus will still be lost.

So many times while my kids were growing up people would comment, "Well, they're good kids." Somehow, we want to believe that church kids are incapable of getting involved in sin or of having ulterior motives when getting together. We must spend time with our kids and strive to know their friends, outside of the church *and* inside. In my experience of raising three girls in the church, church friends were sometimes my biggest challenge. I tried to teach my children that not everyone sitting on a pew in church actually lives what is preached when no one else is watching. Parents should not feel bad about saying "no" to activities if something in their spirit is questioning what is going on.

For one whole summer I did not allow my girls to engage in some outings with our youth group, because I felt like something wasn't right. I had no concrete proof of what was taking place, but I just did not feel good about the frequent gatherings. They claimed to be playing softball or meeting at the church for prayer meetings. How harmful could that be? Later on, however, we learned that some things were not as they seemed. I thank God for giving me discernment. We need to pray for discernment and wisdom as we raise our children, because it is too big of a job for us to handle on our own.

If we do not diligently teach our children, someone else will teach them, and we will raise a generation that knows not God. Raising children in a stable home that knows Truth can surely be a good thing, but just exposing our children to Truth and just setting boundaries for them will not mean a thing to your child. Without revelation and relationship with Jesus Christ, our children will become empty vessels and easy prey for the adversary.

"The thief cometh not, but for to steal, and to kill, and to destroy: I am come that they might have life, and that they might have it more abundantly." (John 10:10)

I was a perfect example of being an empty vessel who fell prey to the enemy at an early age. I realize that I was not raised in or around Truth; nonetheless, I lacked true revelation and relationship. Drinking, partying, smoking cigarettes, and partaking in other sinful behavior became a weekly weekend event for me by the age of fifteen. For a time, I thought I had life by the tail. I had fun friends; we went to some great parties. But, like all sin, not every drunken night ended happily, nor did I wake up every morning thinking I had done the right thing. Many mornings I woke up not even remembering if I drove myself home or not due to the amount of alcohol I had consumed. I would remember the beginning of the evening but not the end, even when my friends would try to clue me in. I was *"choosing...to enjoy the pleasures of sin for a season," (Hebrews 11:25)* but the season was having more downs than ups and more embarrassment, regret, and shame than I would like to share.

Many nights, I lay in bed with tears flowing down my cheeks, wishing I could undo some of the brainless things I had done, but there was no remedy. Even now, knowing I have been forgiven, I still wince at the loathsome memories that have not been erased. Many times I would vow to never get drunk again and would even desperately pray to God, but I would soon find myself right back where I had started.

"As a dog returneth to his vomit, so a fool returneth to his folly." (Proverbs 26:11)

It was the winter of my senior year of high school that I started dating Todd Pace, the man who would become my husband. He was an attractive, quiet, young man who was seen but not often heard at our parties. We had been casual friends throughout high school and were often at the same weekend hot spots; however, our backgrounds could not have been more different.

My husband came and went quite freely from his home. In contrast, even though I was a wild child, I had a father at home that expected some things out of me, and I tried not to disappoint him. He had strict dating and curfew rules in my teen years, so I learned at a young age how to get away with mischief without him finding out. I also noticed that my husband called his parents by their first names. I would not dare call my parents by their first names. The only thing Todd and I had in common, besides a mutual attraction, was the beverage we held in our hand.

The summer after I graduated, Todd and I started to spend most of our free time together, primarily partying with our friends. I recognized that we had differing viewpoints on life matters, including the importance of regular church attendance, family relationships, and money. I thought my viewpoint was right, which meant, of course, his way must be way off base. For example, all Todd was doing that summer was attending guards one weekend a month. He didn't have a regular job. He needed a vehicle. He had dropped out of college. He spent all his time and what little money he had on drinking and fishing. This situation troubled my dad who would say, "That boy needs a job."

That fall, after I had expressed my concern to Todd about his lack of a job, he put an ad out for selling firewood. He would drive down to the river bottoms and chop wood and sell it by the truck load. He worked hard and saved enough money for a down payment on a little Ford truck. When he turned 21, my dad hired him to work at the liquor store he owned. Even though he now had a job and a vehicle, I grew irritated that he seemed to lack the drive to better himself. One day, I told him he needed to get a career path figured out and go back to school or I wasn't sticking around.

My husband was always a good student and school came easy to him, so I couldn't understand why he was so unmotivated. In the meantime, I was also trying to figure out what I wanted to do with my life. I worked full-time at one of our local hospitals, and after looking into various career options, I decided to enroll at a local business college and take some legal secretary courses. Todd, after looking at my career guide, decided to re-enroll at our state college in the Medical Lab Technician program. It was only a two-year program, and he felt he would enjoy the science and math it required. We now both seemed to have a plan, yet I had so many doubts about spending the rest of my life with this guy. We just didn't think alike in so many major areas of our lives.

I broke up with Todd several times while we were dating and once while we were engaged. Devastation would always drive him to do whatever he could to bring us back together. I struggled with guilt because of our relationship, but I also knew that I did not want to go from one relationship to another. So, I finally decided to just stick it out, and I married him.

Chapter Two
Marriage Woes and Lows

On July 1, 1988, Todd and I were married. Todd had just completed his two-year Lab Technician program and had started an evening job at the hospital. He still worked a few hours selling liquor at my parents' liquor store, and he still pulled guard weekend once per month. Meanwhile, I had finished with my secretary training and had landed a job transfer into the hospital's business office.

Todd worked evenings and I worked days, so I decided to get an evening job at our mall in one of my favorite stores. I quickly made friends with the girls I worked with, and we all decided to go out one night after work for drinks. The bar was conveniently attached to the mall. At first it seemed like a harmless night out with friends, but it did not take long until it escalated into an almost nightly routine. Of course, I could not just go to the bar and drink water, and I could never drink just one.

Soon I was drunk more nights than I was sober. My little drinking group became known by all the bartenders, bouncers, and regulars. In fact, we came so regularly that they quit charging us the door fee. Though we were the life of the party, every night I would drive home with confetti in my hair, go to bed, and wake up feeling wrung out. Regardless of how I felt the next morning, I would put my dress clothes on and head out the door to my job at the hospital.

The first few months of marriage seemed to be going great; I even remember thinking that marriage was so much better than dating. However, my nightly bar trips were taking a toll on my conscience. I knew that these months of partying were propelling me down the wrong road quickly. My upbringing taught me enough to know that a young, married woman had no business socializing at a bar, especially without her husband. Todd also drank on a nightly basis, but unlike me, he did not have to have others with him to do so. Believe it or not, his drinking at home irritated me! I thought, "He must have an even bigger problem with drinking than I do. Who drinks alone? *Real* alcoholics drink alone."

I was beginning to realize, though, that my alcohol consumption was also spiraling out of control. My wild times turned into nightmares. The nightlife lost its luster in my life. On the outside, I appeared to be having a good time, but on the inside, I was looking for a way out. During the day at work, I would find myself praying to God to help me. I remember one particular evening as I sat with a drink in my hand and watched all the stupidity taking place on the dance floor, I thought, "Is this really all life has to offer for a good time? I don't belong here. I don't even know why I'm here again." I prayed to God, promising Him that if I got pregnant I would quit going to the bar. I felt like I needed an excuse to stop this harmful cycle I was in.

Much to my amazement, in October of 1988, I found out I was expecting our first child. God had heard the prayer I prayed while sitting on a barstool in that dark, sin-filled atmosphere. I kept my promise and quit attending our nightly drinking rituals. I also quit my evening job, recognizing that I now had a little life to protect. The alcohol I consumed before I knew I was pregnant was a continuing source of worry for me.

One night, while I sat on the couch in our little basement apartment, I opened up my Bible and tried to read from it. It was so hard for me to comprehend at the time, but I desired to know more. I prayed that evening and told the Lord, "If this child is healthy, I will raise it to know You," not knowing the depth of what I prayed or what it would mean for that promise to be fulfilled. Looking back, I realize that even when I did not know God, He was there. He heard my prayers. The Lord began to weave mercy and grace into my life from that time forward.

Pregnancy helped alter some of my life choices for the better, but my marriage went from six months of bliss into a frenzy of fighting and disappointment. Over the three-year stretch of our dating and engagement period, I often had temper blow-outs, behaving in a way that would have driven anyone else to just say, "Forget this! It's not worth it!" My husband, however, would try everything he could to make me happy, because he feared I would just walk the other way. He never showed any angry outbursts toward me; thus, I always felt I had the upper hand in the relationship. But, the young suitor who had once endured my "my way or the highway attitude" disappeared. He was no longer patient with me, and he began to display his anger in a way I would have never expected. He wasn't just disgruntled with me; his temper would rage.

We were only married a short six months when one evening he unleashed his temper. I do not even know what we were fighting about, but within minutes our tiny little apartment became a war zone. My husband called me names (that I will not record) as he destroyed our apartment. He threw my clothes out of the closet, and then he went for my wicker stand which housed a collection of Precious Moments© figurines that I had received over the years from family, friends, and even Todd. The wicker tower came tumbling down, shattering much of my collection. This ended the fight. I sat in silence, observing the destruction and wondering what I had gotten myself into. I was now three months pregnant.

We did not speak to each other for the rest of the evening. I picked up the broken pieces and salvaged what I could. My husband never apologized out loud for what had happened and neither did I. However, I do remember hearing him quietly sniffle as we lay in the dark that night in bed, so I knew he felt bad for what had happened. For the remainder of my pregnancy, we seemed to pull it together. I thought maybe it would never happen again.

Chapter Three
Baby Arrives

While preparing for our first child, I had an overwhelming desire to know more about God and what I believed. I took church attendance on Sundays seriously and tried to get something out of each visit. I just felt like there had to be more to life, and somehow, I knew that I needed more of God.

My department at the hospital worked closely with the collections department, and I was told by my coworkers that the accounts collector, a kind and gentle-spirited man named Mike Chuppe, was in some strict religion. Because I considered myself somewhat religious, I was curious about this, and we did talk about the Lord briefly on a few occasions.

Over time I got to know him and his wife, Shirley, better, and they were always so kind to me. In May, they invited me to a revival service at their church. I didn't really want to go, but I also couldn't say no to them. That evening I arrived at the little, white Apostolic church they attended. I was nervous and unsure of what to expect, as I had never really even heard of being Pentecostal before. My dad once got angry at me for attending the Lutheran church with my soon to be sister-in-law, so I knew he certainly wouldn't approve of me attending the Pentecostal church if he heard about it.

When the service started, people were singing, clapping, and raising their arms high in the air. My mother was involved with a Catholic charismatic group, so I had some exposure to this more exuberant type of worship. I wasn't impressed with the charismatic meetings, and honestly, I wasn't all that impressed with what was going on in this little, white church, either.

The preacher eventually brought the service to a close and made his plea for us to come to the front of the church. Shirley asked me if I wanted to go up and pray. Trying to be polite, I went to the front, knelt down, and closed my eyes, hoping it would be over soon. I remember people laying their hands gently on my shoulder and praying for me. When we finally finished, they asked me what I thought and out loud I said, "It was nice." Inside, I was thinking, "Better you than me!" I was relieved when I walked out the church door, and I had no intentions of ever returning.

On June 17, 1989, McKenzi Elizabeth arrived. She was a beautiful, seven-pound, one-ounce, baby girl with a bed of downy, black hair that hung a bit over her ears. And, she was healthy, an answer to my prayer!

I poured myself into motherhood, loving every minute of it. Todd still worked full-time evenings as a Lab Technician and pulled guard duty one weekend a month. He also made the decision to return to college and finish his degree as a Medical Technologist. Todd worked hard, trying to get us ahead in life; however, when he had free time, spending it with his family was not the activity of choice. He spent his time hunting, fishing, and drinking with his buddies. When I voiced disapproval of his absence, the fights would erupt into name calling and the occasional destruction of things we owned.

With every disagreement or squabble, I became more and more distant from my husband. He did not seem interested in anything I had to say and was often short and impatient. Even when he couldn't find something, he would find a way to blame me for the missing item.

I did not want to spend my life like this, and I did not want to raise our baby in an environment of fighting and yelling at one another. But, I also knew that my parents would be so disappointed that I would even contemplate divorce after making a vow of marriage. So I stayed, while the chasm between us continued to grow.

26

Chapter Four
The Pivotal Moment

Because we needed the second income, I returned to work after my maternity leave ran out. I was blessed to have a close friend watch McKenzi for me on work days, but I could tell by my husband's comments that he disliked this arrangement. My friend even mentioned his unfriendly behavior toward her on the few occasions that Todd picked McKenzi up from daycare. He acted like he was jealous of any friend I had that was outside of our circle of mutual friends. But, in spite of his negativity, I was thankful to have someone I could trust taking care of our baby.

This unpredictable behavior transferred to my family as well. He would sometimes refuse to go with me to family functions, but when he did attend I was often embarrassed and on edge. He behaved gruffly toward my parents or simply ignored them altogether. I tried to act like I didn't notice, but inside I boiled with anger over his immature and rude behavior. In reverse, however, he expected me to be at all of his family gatherings and would have become irate if I ever tried to play the same game he played with my family. Sometimes, to hurt him the way he hurt me, I wanted to treat his family the way he treated mine, but I just couldn't do it. His family had always been good to me. The animosity developing between the two of us was not their fault.

Back at work, with my growing desire to know God, I found myself praying in the bathroom on my breaks, asking Him to help me. The misery in my relationship at home had me longing to find out what life was really all about. I had not found answers in partying, in drinking, or even in my marriage, and I was unsettled and restless. A part of me wanted to run from it all, yet I knew I had nowhere to go to receive the answers I longed for.

I was completely unaware of the Potter's hand of mercy as He began to apply pressure in different areas of my life, continually moving me in the right direction. I remember attending Midnight Mass on Christmas Eve with my sister-in-law, my husband, and one of my husband's brothers. Todd and his brother were inebriated, and thankfully, they stayed at the back of the church. That night, for the first time that I can remember in all my years of attending mass, something the priest said ministered to me. God was starting to get my attention.

At the beginning of the year 1990, my dad checked into the hospital for a back surgery. He had developed a limp a few months earlier when he stepped into a hole and it was assumed that he had merely re-injured his back. After receiving multiple cortisone shots, his condition did not improve, so he consulted with the doctor and decided on surgery. The night before his scheduled surgery day, they performed a routine chest x-ray.

I still remember that I was at home cleaning supper dishes when my mom called me to tell me that my dad's back surgery had been canceled. They had found a spot on my dad's lung that they suspected was cancer, and if so, they would also conclude that the pain in his hip and back was being caused by cancer. I calmly responded, "Ok," but I felt completely numb to what I had just been told. I did not share the news with my husband until the next day, and to my disappointment, his only response was to advise me not to overreact. He never asked any other questions, and he never appeared to be concerned.

My brothers flew home as we waited for the results of the biopsies they had taken from my dad's bone marrow. I will never forget the day the doctor came in and delivered to all of us the grave news of my dad's incurable cancer. I could not imagine life without my dad, the man who always showed us he loved us and always tried to stay involved in our lives. He had been overjoyed to be a grandpa to my daughter, McKenzi, and my oldest brother's daughter, Erica, and now he wouldn't even get to see them grow up.

Unexplainably, when my emotions settled a bit, I slipped into the guest waiting area, picked up the courtesy phone, and dialed the in-house number to my Pentecostal co-worker, Mike Chuppe. The irony that I chose to call him before I even called my closest friends never even entered my mind that day, but clearly, God was compelling me and leading me.

Mike had already heard about my dad's hospitalization, but I relayed to him the devastating news of how the cancer had spread and that they had offered no hope of a cure. He asked me if he and his pastor could come pray for my dad, and I agreed. Later that evening, he and Pastor Walters arrived at the hospital, anointed my dad with oil, and prayed for his healing. They also prayed for our whole family, and we were all touched by their kindness and faith and by this moving experience. As I walked them both back to the elevators to thank them, Mike asked if he and his wife could teach me a Bible study. I agreed.

30

Chapter Five
The Awakening

At the beginning of the first Bible study, I declared allegiance to the Catholic faith, letting my teachers know I had no interest in becoming any other faith, but I learned so much by the end of that first night of study that I couldn't wait until the next lesson! God was opening my eyes to Truth and was lighting my way through His Word. *"Thy word is a lamp unto my feet, and a light unto my path." (Psalm 119:105)* I had an insatiable desire to learn all I could about God's Word, and just like He promised, He began to fill the emptiness and void in my life that I had tried to fill with friends, money, drinking, and the things of this world.

"Blessed are they which do hunger and thirst after righteousness: for they shall be filled." (Matthew 5:6)

In February of 1990, Mike and Shirley again invited me to attend special services at the church. As I recalled my first visit nine months prior, I would never have believed that I would step foot back in that church again. In contrast, on this cold, February evening, I returned with an eagerness to hear the preaching. I had gained a morsel of understanding of God's Word over the past six weeks of Bible study and had been introduced to the Acts 2:38 plan of salvation message.

"Then Peter said unto them, Repent, and be baptized every one of you in the name of Jesus Christ for the remission of sins, and ye shall receive the gift of the Holy Ghost."
(Acts 2:38)

To this day, I vividly recall stepping through the threshold of the swinging doors at the top of the small flight of stairs that lead into the sanctuary of that little church. I felt something I had never felt before in my life, and I immediately began to weep. That night I encountered God's presence, and I went home with excitement and an even greater desire to know God and to be filled with His Spirit.

Because Todd worked evenings, I could attend the services without him interfering. He knew I had been attending the weekly studies, and he certainly did not share my enthusiasm for them. Despite his disdain, however, I knew I had felt the presence of Jesus and nothing could prevent me from knowing Him more. I attended every night of the special services, seeking to be filled with the gift of the Holy Ghost.

At the close of the final service of the revival week, the minister made the invitation to come to the front to pray. I stepped out of my pew and made my way down to the front of the chapel. As people gathered around me to pray, I felt completely immersed by God's presence. However, because we held this Friday night service at a youth correctional center, we had strict time restraints, making it impossible to stay and pray for an unlimited amount of time. Since I was not ready to stop praying, the Chuppes suggested we go to the church and continue to pray there. We stopped by my house to pick up a playpen for McKenzi, and I rode with Shirley over to the church.

Along with the Chuppes, Pastor David Walters and others came to pray with me as I sought to be filled with the Holy

Ghost. I felt God's presence again as we prayed for several hours, but I still was not filled with His Spirit with evidence of speaking in other tongues. Finally, Pastor Walters sat down beside me and spoke to me about the biblical plan of salvation. I told him that I understood repentance and had repented of my sins many times while praying at home. Next, while discussing baptism in Jesus' name, he felt very strongly that if I got baptized, I would receive the Holy Ghost. I made the decision to be baptized in the name of Jesus that night!

By this time, it was already after midnight and eight-month-old McKenzi was fast asleep in the playpen in the church nursery. I changed into a baptismal robe and made my way into the old makeshift baptismal tank that had no heated water. Pastor Walters baptized me in the name of Jesus, and when I came up out of the water, God filled me with the Holy Ghost! Though the water was cold, when the fire of the Holy Ghost entered my life, I no longer even felt the chill of the water. His warm and loving presence surrounded me. My sins were washed away; the old man was dead and gone, and I was given a new life to live.

"Therefore we are buried with him by baptism into death: that like as Christ was raised up from the dead by the glory of the Father, even so we also should walk in newness of life."
(Romans 6:4)

As Shirley drove me home, I got nervous, because I realized that Todd would be home from work by now, probably wondering what in the world I was up to. Knowing I wouldn't be able to hide that my hair was still wet from being baptized, I began to wish that I had driven myself, not wanting Shirley to hear any unkind words from Todd. I hoped he had already gone to bed, but he was up waiting for me. He even opened the front door before I could get out of the car. He stood there, just staring at us as Shirley helped me get the playpen from the trunk. She gave him a friendly wave and said, "Hello." I quickly gathered McKenzi and made my way to the house, hoping he would not say anything ugly until after she left.

When we got inside, he asked, "Why is your hair wet?"

I told him how I had gotten baptized the biblical way, by immersion, and that it was essential to be baptized in Jesus' name to have our sins washed away.

He, thinking I had lost my mind, replied, "You've already been baptized!"

I responded, "But, not the right way!"

I could see his anger and knew he did not want to hear anything I would say, but he just looked at me and said, "I know you are going through a really hard time right now, and you are not thinking right. In time, this will wear off." He thought this was merely a rash reaction to my father's diagnosis of lung cancer, but I knew that I had already made up my mind to live for Jesus. I was not planning to quit, even if Todd got angry. Somehow, I knew this was everything I had been looking for, even though I still had a long way to go.

I continued my weekly Bible studies with the Chuppes, and after receiving the Holy Ghost, I felt like God's Word was even more alive! I experienced the joy of Truth being revealed, but I also felt a sting of disappointment. I had wasted so many years receiving a Catholic education, going to church, observing holy days, and praying the rosary, only to find out that these actions had nothing to do with the true Word of God. I do not share my experience to offend anyone of the Catholic faith, realizing that many dedicated and loyal Catholics and non-Catholics alike strive to be Christ-like, but without the Word of God and without following the essential plan of salvation, we can never be good enough to make it to heaven. We must be saved God's way, not man's way.

My background taught me that God existed and that Christ died on a cross for mankind's sin, but I just never knew that we could know Him on a personal level. I thought I couldn't help falling into sin over and over again and believed that one day, as long as I had not committed any mortal type of sin, I would pay my time in purgatory, and God would let me into heaven. Thank God that He not only keeps us from sinning, but that if we do sin, we have an advocate with the Father. The atoning blood of Calvary applied to my life through baptism in Jesus' name will again, upon my repentance, have the power to cover and remove my sin as far as the East is from the West.

"My little children, these things write I unto you, that ye sin not. And if any man sin, we have an advocate with the Father, Jesus Christ the righteous:" (I John 2:1)

Chapter Six
God Hears Simple Prayers

Every Sunday over the next several months, to keep peace with my husband over my new-found faith, I attended the Catholic church in the morning and the Pentecostal church in the afternoon. My husband's nonchalance toward church attendance seemingly disappeared, and for a short time he began attending the Catholic church regularly on Sundays, a drastic change from his previous sporadic attendance which only included holidays and times that conveniently fit his schedule.

My father, still battling cancer and desperately wanting to be healed, traveled to Nashville and Mexico to receive different types of treatments. When he returned, I briefly told my parents about what I was learning in my Bible studies and in the Sunday afternoon church services at the Pentecostal church. I did not know how to tell my dad that the church in which he had raised his family did not preach the Truth, and that he and my mother, a prayerful woman who daily read the Word of God, both needed to be born again the Bible way. This weighed heavily on my mind, especially knowing that my dad did not have long to live if God did not heal him. In my short, immature walk with God and simple, but sincere, prayer life, the Lord began to work on my dad's heart.

One afternoon, I received a phone call from my dad, and he said, "I was watching Charles Stanley today, and did you know that you need to be born again?" I could hardly contain my surprise, and excitedly responded, "Yes!" I then continued to tell him about repentance and water baptism in Jesus' name. He had my mother call Pastor Walters, and he and his lovely wife came to my parents' home and spent several hours with them, talking to them about being born again. They lined them up with Mike and Shirley, who spent many weeks teaching my parents Bible studies.

In May of 1990, both of my parents were baptized in the name of Jesus Christ and had their sins washed away. My mother had already received the Holy Ghost as a charismatic Catholic, but my father still needed to receive it. One morning, he called me because he thought he may have received the Holy Ghost but was not all the way convinced. He stated that when he woke up, he was praying and thought he was talking in a way he did not understand. News travels fast in a small city, and unbeknown to me, a lady that attended this little Pentecostal church had parents who belonged to the same Catholic church as my parents. The lady's mother, hearing that my parents had been baptized in the Pentecostal church, called them out of concern for their salvation. She informed them that the teachings of the Pentecostal church were not right, and she wanted to make sure that my parents didn't intend to leave the Catholic faith. As the news continued to travel, my parents were bombarded with questions and concerns.

My dad, not seasoned or grounded yet in Truth, did not want to be unfaithful to what he had believed all of his life, so he began to question his decision...and mine. At times, he would become aggravated with me over my decision, and his disapproval distressed me. I did not want to disappoint him, but I knew God had lead me to Truth, and I could not turn back, not even for my father. My brothers, primarily my oldest brother, accused me of acting selfishly in changing faiths and hurting my father while he was dying. I certainly did not want to bring my father sadness as his disease progressed, so for a short time, I distanced myself from going to see him in an effort to not upset him. One morning, however, my mom left to run errands, and my father, nervous of being alone in his weakened condition, called me and asked if I would come over to sit with him by his bed. As we visited, the subject of my changing faiths came up again, and I pleaded with him to understand, saying, "Dad, I would not do this to you at this time of your life if I wasn't fully confident that what I was doing was necessary. I love you, but I must be obedient to the Lord first."

40

Chapter Seven
Isolation and Transformation

My decision to live for God not only began to transform me on the inside, it also brought about change in my social life. First, my closest friends, curious about what was happening in my life, allowed me to share with them the plan of salvation. Some of them would kindly question whether everything I was doing was really necessary for salvation, but others just disagreed with me behind my back. In a short time, my formerly large circle of friendships diminished to a small group. My sister and two brothers continued to openly voice their opposition to my decision. I desperately wanted them to understand, but I could not show them through God's Word what had been revealed to me without it all turning into a big argument. I realized that sharing this precious Truth that God had shown me only works if the other party is receptive, not defensive. In addition, my husband's disapproval of my lifestyle change further compounded the communication problems that already existed in our rocky marriage.

Everything dear and familiar to me began to change: my likes and dislikes, my choice of entertainment, the music I listened to, my conversation, the clothes I wore. As God stripped the unnecessary from my life during this process of change, I felt slighted by the closest people in my life who believed I had gone off the deep end. Although they still talked to me at times, our relationships had forever changed, and I could feel the gulf between us. I experienced times of loneliness that drew me to a place of prayer for comfort; however, during the shedding of my old self, the Lord added a church family that supported me and reached out to me to make me feel welcome.

Also, the Lord began to establish me through Bible study and worship services. *"For precept must be upon precept, precept upon precept; line upon line, line upon line; here a little, and there a little:" (Isaiah 28:10)* I knew that I did not want to be a halfway Christian, and although I saw the necessity of the plan of salvation and believed in the oneness of God, I still had some questions about God's expectations of the way I dressed. Every time I had a question about what to do or why it should be done, God would answer me through the preached Word of God. For example, I had been attending church for six or seven months and had not fully committed to wearing dresses like the other ladies in the Pentecostal church. I understood the need to be more modest in what I selected to wear, but I was not convinced I needed to get rid of my pants. One evening, during one of my weekly Bible studies with the Chuppes, we had a discussion on ladies' attire. They handled my questions wisely and suggested that I talk with Pastor Walters on the subject, but at that time I did not know him well enough to feel comfortable broaching this subject with him. To my amazement, the very next Sunday Pastor Walters preached an excellent message of holiness and separation. He briefly covered the scripture on ladies' modesty, and he used a scripture out of the book of Deuteronomy. *"The woman shall not wear that which pertaineth unto a man, neither shall a man put on a woman's garment: for all that do so are abomination unto the LORD thy God." (Deuteronomy 22:5)*

I knew God had spoken directly to me, and I had to decide to which level I would commit my life to Him. I went home and packed up every pair of pants I owned, because I decided to trust and obey God's Word, even though I did not understand it all clearly. Obedience to God always brought joy, and when I obeyed, He proceeded to open my understanding. *"Trust in the LORD with all thine heart and lean not unto thine own understanding. In all thy ways acknowledge him and he shall direct thy paths." (Proverbs 3:5-6)*

God began to deal with me regarding my hair as well. Todd did not like short hair, and when we got engaged and set our wedding date, he asked that I grow my hair out for our wedding. Even with longer hair, I was the girl always looking for a new hairdo or hair color. Right before being saved, I had this crazy idea to chop my hair off above my ears, having no idea what the Word of God had to say on the subject. I seemed to be losing my hair in handfuls after McKenzi turned about six months old, so I thought shorter hair would make this hormone change easier. I never mentioned to Todd my intention to cut my hair, and he came home that night from work, got into bed, and when he reached his arm around me, he jumped back out of bed and turned the light on, exclaiming, "What did you do to your hair? Yuck! I thought I was sleeping with a guy!"

At the time, I retorted, "It's not your hair so don't worry about it!" But, when I got saved and saw in God's Word that I needed to grow my hair out, I remembered that night and laughed that my husband, without knowing the Word of God, knew that my hair should be long.

"Doth not even nature itself teach you, that, if a man have long hair, it is a shame unto him? But if a woman have long hair, it is a glory to her: for her hair is given her for a covering." (I Corinthians 11:14-15)

I am aware that my outward appearance alone does not save me, but when a life in ruins encounters the Savior, Jesus Christ, through repentance, water baptism in His name, and the infilling of the Holy Ghost, transformation occurs from the inside out. Through months of struggles, trials, and temptations, God always pulled me through. I knew Him as a Savior, but through prayer, He became my Shield and Buckler, my Prince of Peace, my Counsellor, my heavenly Father, and my closest Friend. He was the Potter, and I was the clay, and although it sometimes hurt as He molded me and shaped me, I knew He would never leave me or forsake me, and I could trust Him.

He is still the Potter and I am still the clay, and He continues to mold me and make me after His will. I want my life to be a reflection of His holiness, His goodness, and His mercy, so I can be pleasing to Him. I am thankful for a life of holiness and separation that has spared me from so much sorrow since making the decision to live for Jesus.

Chapter Eight
Continued Trials

On September 25, 1990, I received a phone call around 5:00 a.m. that my father had passed away in the hospital. I had been with him just a few hours before and had wrestled with whether I should work the next day or stay with him, not knowing if he would hang on for another day. I finally decided to go home, and to this day, I regret that decision.

When the call came, Todd was up getting ready to go to his early morning classes. Because of our strained relationship, he had not offered much support during the nine months of my dad's illness. I resented his seeming disinterest and made up my mind to not offer him any information or updates, so when he heard me cry out at the news of my dad's death and came offering comfort, I recoiled from his touch and got up to get dressed to go to the hospital. When he offered me a ride, I lashed out and cried, "You haven't been here the last nine months to help me and now you want to give me a ride? I don't need your help!"

So many nights, I agonized over my dad's salvation, wondering if he had received the Holy Ghost and if he had made it to heaven. One night, I had a dream that my dad came to my bedside and thanked me for showing him Truth. I do not know for certain that God gave me that dream, but I have never had a dream about my father like that since that time, and it helped me give the matter of his salvation over to God. He had been baptized in Jesus' name; all his sins had been washed away, and he was now in God's hands.

Shortly after we buried my father, I discovered I was expecting again. Todd was still in college, still working evenings at the lab, and still pulling guard drill once a month. I was now at home putting in long hours as a daycare provider as a means to supplement the family finances while also staying home with McKenzi.

My relationships inside the church grew, but my relationship at home with Todd seemed to dwindle even more. Because of our demanding schedules, we did not have much opportunity to spend time together to repair the strain, but when we did spend time together, we often ended up annoyed with one another or in a fight.

One afternoon, in January of 1991, I was listening to the news regarding the trouble in the Middle East with Iraq and heard that the United States was going to war. Not long after, our phone rang, and a ranking officer from the National Guard requested to speak with my husband. I explained that Todd was in school, and he responded that he needed to speak to Todd, so I needed to have him call back as soon as possible. When Todd returned the phone call, he discovered he was being called to active duty and would have to prepare to leave by that weekend. Our shared disbelief and fear for the future helped us rally together for our little family. He was stationed stateside in Missouri with his unit on standby for medical support overseas, and while he was gone, we kept in touch by phone as often as we could.

With the expected arrival of our second child, I went on a hunt for a small, first-time home we could purchase. My mother and I found a brand new, small home located across from a grade school. It was a perfect starter home for us with a nice yard for children to play, ideal for the daycare I ran during the day. Todd returned home a few weeks before my due date, and I welcomed him home to our new residence, hoping for a fresh start for all of us.

He returned to the Medical Technologist program with only about four weeks left until his Bachelor of Science degree would be completed. He was excited about our new home and quickly got to work leveling dirt and planting grass so the kids could play.

On May 25, 1991, Ashton Michelle Pace arrived! God had blessed us with another beautiful, healthy baby girl with a downy top of black hair. She was born about 5:25 a.m., and by 7:30 or 8:00 a.m., my husband asked if he could go fishing. I was learning it was easier to just agree, even when I resented that he seemed to not understand the value of family. Although I understood that sitting around a hospital room with company and with nurses coming in and out is not on the top-ten list for most men, I still had a hard time processing that he didn't want to be there with us.

The first few weeks of him being home seemed to be running smoothly, but soon the bliss and blessing of being back together blew up into a fit of anger. The day before his Medical Technology graduation, he ransacked our neatly groomed and polished home in a rage, toppling our living room furniture and breaking a few spindles on our new oak stair banister. When the storm passed, he managed to repair the broken spindles, while I cleaned up the other ruins in silence, wishing he had never returned.

The next day, I attended his graduation with our two daughters, and all of Todd's classmates and professors were so complimentary of Todd's beautiful family. I put my best smile on and pretended we were the perfect, all-American family.

My husband had a brilliant mind, and he graduated in the top one percent in the nation for his field of occupation. He heard about a supervisory position for a lab at a satellite clinic to one of our major hospitals, so he applied and was hired. He now worked all daytime hours with no weekends, and usually put in enough time Monday through Thursday to even take every Friday off. Now that he no longer had to go to school all day and work all evening, it seemed his stress would decrease; however, the adjustment of having him home during the evenings was not easy, increasing the frequency of our fights. Also, I no longer had the evening to myself for prayer, so I had to readjust to the early morning hours.

Our home was very tense most of the time. I would do daycare all day, and as soon as Todd got home from work, I felt as if I were walking on eggshells. He lost his temper and raised his voice over so many things, and when he was mad about something, he would often pretend he was bowing to me. If I ever said anything, he would respond with, "Oh, holy one, you're so much better than I am," and would often call me derogatory names for being Pentecostal. He referred to the church people as "goongahs."

With each offense, I built higher walls. I got to a point where I only talked with him on an as-needed basis, acting pleasant but indifferent toward him. I wanted God to change him but nothing was changing, and with every fiber of my being I wanted out of this hopeless relationship. I struggled with guilt for feeling this way, fearing I would make the wrong decision and be just as lost and hopeless as him. At times, because of prayer, church, and strength from God's Word, I would get a handle on my resentment and would try to love my husband like I should, resulting in a normal, functioning relationship for fleeting periods of time.

I became numb to the tirades that often took place and would usually just sit and watch as my husband destroyed our belongings, yelling and cursing at me. Sometimes I just stared at him in disbelief over the destruction he caused in our own home. During one angry episode, my husband tore the blinds off of our windows and ripped up my Bible. We were not wealthy, and though the blinds were not expensive or custom-made, it was a sacrifice to have to go out and purchase new ones. I struggled with having to pull everything together and with having to act like everything was just as it should be, and although I did not outwardly rage back at my husband, inside I struggled with bitterness over all the hurts and shattered dreams.

I just wanted a normal family that spent family time together without bickering and a normal husband who considered a day playing outside with the kids time well spent. All I could see was a husband who would rather hunt, fish, and drink beer with his friends on the weekend. When given a choice over what he would rather do, I could attest that we were not the first pick.

During these troublesome times, I continued to pray, attend church, and even teach some Bible studies. Todd still did not accept my lifestyle, but he never forbade me from going to church. He also never stood in the way of our children attending with me. I believe the Lord used Todd's desire to not be strapped down in the evenings and on Sundays as a way to ensure our children could always attend church with me.

Most weekends, Todd would leave the house on a Saturday morning for guard drill or for a day of hunting or fishing, and he would just not return home until he had drunk his fill at the bar with his friends. Many times, I would hunt him down and call him at the bar because I had made supper, expecting him home, or because he had said he would watch the kids so I could go shopping on my own for the afternoon. Even though he didn't come home when I called, I wanted him to know that he was rude for not calling, and that I recognized his double standard.

He always expected me to show up exactly at the time I told him, or he would fly into a rage, but it seemed he did not feel the need to return the courtesy.

I do not want to paint the picture of a man who never had remorse over his actions, because he did. He would apologize, promising to not lose his temper like that anymore or promising to quit drinking so much, but he just had no power to keep his promise. I knew he lacked the power, because I remembered lacking it myself, but I wanted to believe him and wanted him to turn his life over to God. I agonized with God in prayer for what we needed, often begging the Lord to change and save my husband, but it seemed the more I prayed, and the harder I tried to draw closer to the Lord, the harder my life became.

I made a commitment to prayer early on in my walk with God. At a Sunday afternoon church service, a traveling evangelist, Brother McDaniel, preached that the greatest sin we can commit as Christians is to not pray. I felt a sting in my spirit and conviction that I needed a deeper and more consecrated prayer life, so I made a promise that day to pray. I was not blessed with many outward talents but knew I could learn to pray, so on my knees in my bedroom I spent time with God in prayer. That message about prayer still rings in my ears today and pushes me to pray.

The devil tried to thwart my prayer life, discourage me, and even scare me. I knew very little about attacks from Satan, because this was all new to me, but I had several nights where it felt as if someone was trying to suffocate me during the night. Once, after praying and going to bed for the night, an oppressive spirit filled my room, and although I was asleep, it was as if I was awake, and I could feel this deep, weighty presence. I could also see McKenzi, barely two years old, standing in her crib, and this presence would not let me go get her to protect her. In my dream, I reached for my Bible and tried to give it to McKenzi, but it was whisked out of my hand. I struggled against this oppressive feeling in my sleep, trying with all my might to call on Jesus. Finally, I was able to say, "JESUS!" Immediately, the ugly spirit I felt left my room, and the presence of God flooded around me. When I awoke, I was sitting straight up in bed speaking loudly in tongues. I quickly shut my mouth and lay back down, hoping my husband had not noticed, because to my knowledge, he had never heard me or anyone else speak in tongues.

The next day, I went over the dream in my mind, and I could not get over how real it felt. I shared it with a friend from the church who said it could very well have been real, so when Todd came home for lunch, I stepped out and mentioned to him that I had a really bizarre dream the night before. I explained that I felt a creepy presence in our room, and he looked at me and said, "I don't want to talk about it." When I asked him why, he stated, "I felt it, too." That was the end of our conversation, but I knew then that the enemy was not happy with me praying. Instead of stopping me, this knowledge caused me to be more determined about praying, and I began to read books by people like Joy Haney on prayer and fasting.

52

Chapter Nine
The Decade of Despair

In June of 1992, the discovery that I was expecting our third child caused mixed emotions. I loved my children, but I struggled with rearing them virtually on my own in the midst of a rocky marital relationship. I told Todd the news while he was at guard training in California and was puzzled by his positive reaction, considering he was an uninvolved parent most of the time. My mixed emotions about having another baby were short lived, however, and I was soon looking forward to adding a newborn to the mix. On February 10, 1993, God blessed us with another beautiful baby girl, London Nicole.

The Christmas before she was born, I asked Todd if he would keep the kids so I could go shopping with a girlfriend for a Saturday. I rarely infringed on him to do this for fear of a fight, but I was pregnant and wanted to get my holiday shopping done without the kids. Besides that, he had been hunting and out drinking excessively for weeks while I had been at home taking care of the kids. He agreed to watch them for me but when the set weekend came, he arrived home late on Friday night from hunting and drinking and mentioned that the guys wanted him to go out hunting again in the morning. I reminded him of his promise to watch the kids for my shopping day and informed him I would not change my plans. I could tell that this upset him, but he did not immediately respond. This lasted only until we went to bed that night, and then he began to complain to me about not getting to go hunting in the morning. I tried to ignore him and just go to sleep, but he started to kick at me with his foot to get my attention. Each time, I moved closer to my edge of the bed, and although he was not kicking me hard enough to hurt me, I knew he was trying to start a fight. I finally slipped out of bed and exited our bedroom, hoping he would not follow. Thankfully, he left me alone, and I slept away from him on our downstairs couch.

When Todd got angry he would break things and verbally assault me, but he was getting close to the edge of physical abuse when he would periodically grab me firmly in anger. I almost could not bear the stress of having him home, and sadly, having him gone at work or out with his friends was actually a respite from the tension of his unpredictable behavior. I never wanted my kids to feel insecure by being exposed to these foolish fights, so I did my best to avoid confrontation when they were awake. I also always tried to make holidays, birthdays, and family gatherings a special time, purposefully avoiding any irritations that would upset my husband and cause a disturbance.

This up and down, yo-yo type relationship was wearing me out, and as our troubles escalated, I wondered if staying in this marriage would cause my children to grow up with a skewed perception of marriage and family. I had Apostolic friends who exemplified strong marriages and homes, and more than anything, I desired those things for my children.

Hunting season seemed to be a volatile time of year for us, and in the fall of 1993, a common friend of ours witnessed one of Todd's outbursts. The few friends that we had from high school and our dating years thought my husband was a mild-mannered guy, so when I had disclosed to our common friend some of the problems we had been having, she sympathized but didn't quite believe that he was as out of hand as I was describing. Now, with her eyewitness account of his anger, she was in utter disbelief that this was the same man she had known in high school. Seeing him through her eyes woke me up, and I made up my mind that I could not stay. McKenzi was now four; Ashton was two, and London was about eight months old.

Todd got up early the next morning to go hunting, and I feigned sleep while I waited for him to leave the house. When I heard him leave, I waited a few minutes to make sure he had driven away and then got up, pulled some suitcases out of storage, and began to pack clothes for the kids and me to escape. When the three girls awoke, I fed them, got them dressed, made the beds and picked up the house. I wanted it to appear as normal as possible so my husband would not immediately suspect our absence.

My closest friend from church met me at another friend's house to help me make a plan, because beyond leaving, I really had not decided what to do. I feared that I had made the wrong decision, yet I did not want to continue in this unhealthy relationship. Right away, my friend insisted I call our pastor. I knew I needed to call him but was afraid of what he would say. He already knew most of my situation and how Todd did not support my involvement in the church, yet he listened to me and seemed to understand that I was at my wit's end. He assured me that he would be in prayer for our family and suggested that perhaps my departure would give Todd a spiritual wake-up call. Next, although my mom was out of town, I called her to ask if I could stay at her house until I could get Todd removed from our home.

When Todd arrived home after a long day of hunting, he did not know what had taken place. We had not spoken to each other since the upheaval the day before, but I'm sure he probably assumed we would carry on as usual; he would give me space, and I would get over it. However, when it started to get late, and I still had not returned, alarms must have started going off in my husband's head. He called around looking for me, but no one seemed to know where I had gone. He started calling my church phone list, eventually calling Pastor Walters, who tried to talk to my husband about our situation. Todd flew off the handle, cussed my pastor out, and hung up, wanting to blame the church for our problems.

Todd left the house, frantically trying to find us, and finally ended up at my mom's door. By this time, the kids were sound asleep, and when he came to the door, I refused to let him in. He started swearing at me and banging on the door, so I called my friend who directed me to immediately call 911. The dispatcher kept me on the phone until the officers arrived, and after they made sure Todd left, they suggested I go somewhere else and took me to a friend's home for the night. Todd called his parents in distress, and they, worried about his state of mind, sent the authorities to check on him. The police felt like he needed to go to the Psyche Ward for overnight observation, but he was released immediately the following morning.

The next day, I went to my friend's home in Mandan, and Todd once again started searching for us. He found us at their home and knocked on the door, insisting he talk to me. My friend and her husband hid us in a bedroom and politely asked him to leave, but from behind the door of the bedroom, I could hear his angry refusal. They called the authorities, and when they arrived, my husband drove away peaceably. The authorities took us to a safe house, because I did not want to keep putting my friends in the middle of our problems. It took a day and a half to get an attorney, file for a legal separation, and have my husband removed from our home.

I had been praying about our marriage for what seemed like such a long time now, but nothing had changed. I loved God and wanted to do things His way. I wanted to live for Him. I wanted my children to live for Him. I wanted Him to save my husband. It seemed so impossible! I could quote the scripture, *"For with God nothing shall be impossible," (Luke 1:37)* and I truly believed that *nothing* was impossible...except maybe our marriage.

My husband, desperate to get us back, called Pastor Walters, apologized for what he had said to him on the phone, and even set up an appointment to meet with him. Pastor Walters called to let me know Todd had apologized and asked me to pray about his meeting with my husband. I couldn't believe what I was hearing! Maybe, just maybe, this was going to be our answer.

While we were apart, Todd promised to quit drinking, to quit the verbal abuse, and to quit flying off the handle and destroying everything in his path. He vowed to be a better family man by spending quality time with us and agreed to let Pastor Walters give us marriage counseling.

Amidst these promises, I eventually let my husband return home. We continued for a little while longer in counseling and started designating family nights with the kids and date nights for ourselves without the kids. I felt like we had a new lease on life, but our time of peace ended quickly as we slipped right back into our old routine.

Todd started drinking every night, and his fuse remained short. I built up bigger walls and was feeling indifferent toward him; however, I made it very clear to my husband that going forth, I would not tolerate his explosive and abusive behavior, and I would not tolerate him wrecking our home.

A few years passed after our short separation, and late in November one year, I put up our beautiful, full-foliaged, artificial Christmas tree. The kids and I adored the Christmas season and had spent hours decorating the tree. When we finished, I tucked the munchkins into bed and cleaned the house. All was well.

Todd returned that evening from a long day of hunting with his friends. In complete shock, I watched as he became unhappy for some unknown reason, and in seconds, went from making snide comments to exploding in anger. I did not say a word because I did not want to prolong his outburst or wake up the kids, but before I knew what had happened, our beautifully decorated tree was flung to the floor! The decorations scattered across the living room as I heard a small voice at the top of the stairs asking why daddy threw the tree down. I quickly went to our oldest daughter, scooped her up, and headed back downstairs to her room, trying to evade her question. I really did not know why a grown man would do such a thing, so I had no words to tell her. Todd went to bed and got up the next morning to continue his hunting weekend.

Lying awake in the basement that night, I replayed the events of the evening, agonizing over so much destruction in such a short amount of time. I then started thinking of all his other similar explosions and wondered if I could continue like this. How could this be the best atmosphere to raise our children? How could I instill into them the Truth and how Christians should live while subjecting them to hell on earth in our own home?

That weekend, I again made the decision to leave. The kids and I checked into a hotel where I knew my husband could not find us. My stomach was in knots from the fear of making an eternal mistake. I tried to pray, but my strength and faith were weak. I would get waves of nausea and run to the bathroom with dry heaves from all the stress of the battle raging in my own heart. I knew the devastating effects of divorce on children and wanted them to have the security of a mother and father who loved and cared for them, but I also wanted them to have the privilege of growing up with parents who lived for God, which didn't seem like a reality for us. I moved in with my mom, separating from my husband for the second time.

Eventually, Todd persuaded me to come back home, promising once again that he would change. However, sometime during that separation, I made a decision to stop praying for God to change my husband. I realized that not only could I not change him, unless Todd decided to surrender his will, God also could not change him. If I wanted our marriage to work, *I needed to change.*

I was *miserable,* so I prayed for myself, asking God to change *me.* I needed to forgive my husband and let go of all the bitterness and resentment that I had bottled up against him, because whether he deserved forgiveness, I knew this bitterness was robbing my joy. I asked God to help me love my husband as he was, not as I wanted him to be and to help me be the wife I needed to be for my husband. I prayed for godly wisdom and understanding, asking the Lord to help me see through His eyes and not my own, so that my husband could see the Lord in me.

"Likewise, ye wives, be in subjection to your own husbands; that, if any obey not the word, they also may without the word be won by the conversation of the wives;"
(I Peter 3:1)

From that time forward, the mood and atmosphere in our home began to change. It was a slow process, but with lots of fervent prayer and time spent with God, I was able to forgive and let go of all the hurt and disappointments I had encountered in our relationship. I spent most of the first ten to eleven years of our marriage on the Potter's wheel as His hands began to mold me and shape me, chipping away and smoothing my rough edges and putting me through the fire.

> *"Then I went down to the potter's house, and, behold, he wrought a work on the wheels. And the vessel that he made of clay was marred in the hand of the potter: so he made it again another vessel, as seemed good to the potter to make it."*
> *(Jeremiah 18:3-4)*

I want to say that I do not condone verbal or physical abuse, and I did draw a clear line with my husband on these issues when he slipped back into a rage of destruction one last time. He came home after being out drinking and went to the fridge, looking for some leftovers that I had already discarded. He began to rant about me throwing out everything and accused me of being wasteful.

I had just finished making filling for stuffed peppers for the following evening, because I had invited my aunt and uncle over to have dinner with the kids and me while Todd worked late. In his anger, he took my freshly cooked filling and turned on our disposal and began to dump the filling into the sink. I told him to stop and reached for the kettle, but he blocked me, picked me up roughly, and held me against the cupboards. McKenzi, eleven years old at the time, saw what was taking place and immediately sprang into action. She grabbed our kitchen broom and came at my husband, warning him to back away. He stopped immediately.

I left with the kids and went back to my mom's house, completely shocked that this had happened again. I knew God had given us victory in this area! But, Todd's remorse was different this time, and he did not make empty promises. He was humiliated that McKenzi felt like she had to protect me, and he knew his actions were out of line. I let him know that manhandling me in the future would not be tolerated, and he said, "If I ever get out of line like that again, you won't have to leave. I will." For some reason, I knew he meant what he said. He owned up to his actions and knew he was completely responsible for how he had acted.

From that time forward, my husband did not destroy another thing in our home and never grabbed me out of anger again. It did not completely alleviate his temper, but he somehow began to channel his anger without all the destruction. More than anything, God was at work.

Chapter Ten
A Foundational Miracle

In the midst of this conflict, I often felt like the struggle would never end; peace and solitude were nowhere to be found. Each day began to feel like a time warp with no chance of moving forward and no possibility of going back to better days. However, things were changing, even though some of the changes were so subtle that it took me a while to realize just how far God had brought us over the last ten years. Our marriage still had flaws, of course, and the spiritual division between us still existed, but God was doing a work. He was preparing me, preparing my husband, and protecting and keeping our children.

"Commit Thy way unto the LORD; trust also in him; and he shall bring it to pass." (Psalm 37:5)

My advice for any man or woman living with an unsaved spouse is to be committed to the things of God. Be faithful. Seek first His kingdom. I had to learn to submit to my husband in many areas of my life, even when I didn't agree. God intended for my husband to lead our home, whether saved or unsaved, so I submitted to him in any capacity that would not go against the Word of God or compromise any of my God-given convictions regarding separation and holiness. I am happy to report that my husband never tried to get me to go to the bars with him, never asked me to stop wearing dresses, and never asked me why I no longer wore makeup or cut my hair.

Do not bend or take part in sinful activities or compromise what you believe. Even though your spouse may say hurtful things against you for what you believe, hold your ground, not with a negative attitude but with a desire to do what is right and pleasing to God. *"Blessed are ye, when men shall revile you, and persecute you, and shall say all manner of evil against you falsely, for my sake."* *(Matthew 5:11)* God will honor your faithfulness, and with time, your spouse will come to respect and admire your devotion to what you believe, watching to see if what you have is real.

"Let your light shine before men, that they may see your good works, and glorify your Father which is in heaven."
(Matthew 5:16)

As a child, my husband suffered from asthma attacks, some so severe that he had to be hospitalized. When I met Todd, he no longer used any type of asthma medication and seemed to have overcome his attacks through exercise. It was not until after nine or ten years of marriage that I even realized he had asthma, because he never talked about it. I noticed one afternoon, after he came home from jogging, that he was coughing funny and seemed to be struggling to get enough air. I asked him about it, but I could tell he did not want to discuss his condition, as if he were ashamed.

In the spring of 2001, Todd's asthma attacks came on with a vengeance. Most of his asthma attacks occurred in the middle of the night, interrupting our sleep. He got irritable when I would speak to him about the attacks, so I avoided mentioning them unless I felt it was absolutely necessary. I just prayed silently, sometimes gently laying my hand on him in prayer. One evening, his struggle for air was too much, and we ended up in the emergency room. Todd finally gave in and got an inhaler to carry with him, but he was not happy about having to use one again.

Several weeks later, Todd began to cough and wheeze in the middle of the night while I lay still, hoping and praying it would pass. I finally reached over, gently laid my hand on his chest, and silently asked the Lord to stop the coughing. It stopped instantly! I asked God to help him breathe without wheezing. He started to breathe normally! I asked God to let him rest. He fell back to sleep! I could scarcely contain my excitement over the miracle I had just witnessed God perform for my husband through a silent prayer! I lay in bed, silently rejoicing and praising God.

Some might think this miracle seems small, but I believe this answer to prayer touched my husband in more ways than one. The Lord was definitely at work all along in our marriage, but I think this miracle made my husband truly aware of the power of living for God.

The next day, I had to say something to him. I just had to know if Todd realized that God had stepped on the scene in his moment of need. I knew I needed to tread lightly, because any spiritual-sounding conversations were still abruptly shut down, so I light-heartedly said, "Thanks for keeping me awake last night with your asthma attack."

My husband responded, "What asthma attack?"

"Don't act like you don't know that God healed you last night," I replied and proceeded to tell him that when I laid my hand on him and prayed for him, God instantly did everything I asked Him to do.

My husband felt awkward and wasn't quite sure how to respond to me, but he answered, "I know He did."

"You just need to thank Him!" I told him.

As he was walking away to end the conversation, I heard him say, "I already did".

From that time forward, the derogatory name-calling and poking fun of church people and the way we worshipped ceased. Though this miracle did not cause Todd to want to attend church with me or ask more about my convictions, he had a new respect for what I believed. He had witnessed the power of a small, silent prayer and now knew personally that God was a healer! This miracle was a stepping stone to increase our faith for the next decade of our life.

Chapter Eleven
Another Leap in Faith

McKenzi had expressed several times after receiving the Holy Ghost at the age of seven that she wanted to be baptized in Jesus' name. She was sensitive to the things of God and knew she needed to have her sins washed away according to the Acts 2:38 message. My pastor desired for my husband, the spiritual leader of our home, to give McKenzi permission to be baptized, but when we went to ask him, he got upset and abruptly responded, "No!" I asked him one more time privately, and he said, "When she is eighteen she can decide for herself, but until then, no."

When she was eleven years old, McKenzi came to me while I was scrubbing the floor and asked again about being baptized. I told her we needed to ask her dad, and she got upset, fearing he would again say no. I tried to comfort her, but inside I was feeling upset, too.

Later that day, I called my pastor and spoke with him regarding the matter. I explained to him that I understood that Todd was still considered our spiritual leader, but I also added that if I left all the spiritual decisions up to my husband, we probably would not be coming to church any longer. My pastor understood my frustration but wisely suggested, "Let's pray one more time that your husband will consent; if he doesn't, I will let you make the final decision." We prayed in Jesus' name and a few days later, I worked up the nerve to ask him again. I could not believe what I was hearing when he said, "If it means that much to her, then go ahead." I immediately called my pastor, and he recommended that the other two girls, having received the Holy Ghost as well, get baptized in Jesus' name at the same time as McKenzi. What an awesome, prayer-answering God!

In the fall of 2001, my husband and I moved our family to a quaint, three-acre country location with a small, ranch-style home. The yard was surrounded with beautiful trees and various bushes, but the modest home needed much repair and updating. Todd quickly got to work tearing out walls, doors, and kitchen cupboards. He put in forty-plus hour weeks at his daytime job and then came home and worked well past midnight many nights on our numerous remodeling efforts. We still were not equally yoked spiritually, but God was helping us to come together in areas that we could both share. My husband slowly began to support the way the children and I lived but mostly through non-verbal communication.

When we moved to the country, our kids had to change to a different school, causing a lot of stress. They were now the new kids on the block and were also the only Pentecostal kids in the school. During the first week of school, things seemed to be going smoothly until the morning our middle daughter, Ashton, refused to get on the bus and go to school. The bus came and went without her, and not knowing what to do with her defiance, I had no choice but to call my husband who was already at work. He told me to leave for work and to put her on the phone, so I gave the phone to Ashton and left for work.

I soon received a phone call from Todd who explained that Ashton was afraid to go to school because the gym teacher had announced that dresses could not be worn on phy-ed days. Since this was a phy-ed day, Ashton did not want to be pointed out in front of students she barely knew. My heart sank, and I thought, "Here it comes. He's going to chew me out because the girls wear dresses all of the time."

To my surprise, he said, "You get over to that school and talk to those teachers and let them know how it is. You tell them that our girls wear dresses every day, and they will not be singled out because of it! If they don't like it, let me know, and I will pay a visit to the school!"

I hung up and had to rejoice! God again proved He was at work. My husband knew that the way we lived was right, even if he didn't have the biblical knowledge at the time to back it up. God was changing his heart.

I went to the school and visited with her homeroom teacher who assured me that Ashton's dress would not hinder anything at school and that she would discuss it with the gym teacher. We never had one more issue with the dress code for gym class.

Chapter Twelve
Raising Children to Love God

I was told once that very few children who grow up in a home where only one parent serves God continue to live for God once old enough to make their own decisions. I knew the challenges in raising them to live for God without both of us living the same lifestyle, but I would not accept that my children would be lost because of their father's choice. It did not make any sense to me, so I took this matter to the Lord in prayer. The same God who saved me could certainly keep my children! I began to dedicate my children to the Lord on a daily basis and continued to do so, even as they became young adults. They belong to Him!

> *"I have no greater joy than to hear that my children walk in truth." (III John 1:4)*

I also knew that I needed to remain obedient to His Word and faithful in my walk with God. It was not always going to be easy, but with the Lord's help, I was determined to do the best I could to live for God and to put Truth into the hearts of my children.

> *"And thou shalt teach them diligently unto thy children, and shalt talk of them when thou sittest in thine house, and when thou walkest by the way, and when thou liest down, and when thou risest up." (Deuteronomy 6:7)*

The greatest thing I could do for my children was be an example of faithfulness, whether in the valley low or high on the mountain top. At times, my three busy, determined daughters, all close in age, made this task exhausting. Many church services I felt like my three munchkins and I were the main show of a three-ringed circus, and I remember crying on my way home from church, lamenting that I had received no spiritual nourishment from the service. I thought my daughters would never learn; however, with endurance and training, the consistency began to pay off, and I was able to raise my daughters on the church pews.

I also tried to surround my kids with as much Apostolic fellowship as I could. Every year we looked forward to family camp as our summer vacation, and my children began to excitedly discuss the July camp as early as Christmas time. The first few years, my church family helped erect a tent for my girls and me, and we would spend the week of camp enduring violent thunderstorms, wet sleeping bags, sweltering days, and stifling hot church services in a tabernacle with no air conditioning. By the end of the week, I was exhausted physically but refreshed spiritually from a week of Holy Ghost filled services. I delighted in being surrounded by godly fellowship.

"Not forsaking the assembling of ourselves together, as the manner of some is; but exhorting one another: and so much the more as ye see the day approaching." (Hebrews 10:25)

After the first few years of dragging our belongings and coolers by myself, my husband must have begun to feel guilty over other people helping me set up camp. He bought me a large, two-room tent and started driving up in a separate vehicle to help me set up our campsite. He would secure our tent and head back for home, only to return at the end of the week to help me take down our tent and pack up our belongings. He would often call the camp and sound the alarm if a major storm was heading right toward us. It always scared him, because we basically had no communication with the outside world for the whole week. After many years of tenting, my husband blessed us with a camper.

When Todd came to set up camp for us, he would not stay and make conversation with any of the church people at the camp, but God used these encounters to start tearing down the walls around my husband's heart. The Lord helped me to understand and see my husband in a new light. His acts of kindness were his expression of love for the girls and me. Underneath the rough exterior was a man who loved his family, a man who wanted to be closer to us but did not know how to do so.

74

Chapter Thirteen
A Promise in the Night

I attended our district ladies retreat in Minot, North Dakota in May of 2002. Sister Joy Haney was going to be our guest speaker, and knowing her to be a lady of prayer, I went expecting great things. The power of the Holy Ghost filled each session as Sister Haney spoke with anointing on the power of prayer and standing on God's promises. She encouraged me to go deeper in God and reinforced my desire for a more steadfast prayer life when she connected some scriptures together on faith and having what we ask for according to God's will in prayer. *"And this is the confidence that we have in him, that, if we ask ANYTHING according to his will, he heareth us: And if we know that he hear us, whatsoever we ask, we know that we have the petitions that we desired of him." (I John 5:14-15, emphasis added)* To this day I lean on these verses in prayer.

At one point, Sis Haney laid her hands on me and prayed for my husband; I could feel the Holy Ghost descend on me in a powerful way. I came home with a renewed confidence, hope, and determination that God would save my husband. I chose to believe that God was working even when I could not see.

> *"Now faith is the substance of things hoped for, the evidence of things not seen." (Hebrews 11:1)*

My first night back home, May 3, 2002, the Lord woke me up in the middle of the night. I felt His presence so strongly that I slipped out of bed and went into our living room to pray. As I prayed, I grabbed my journal to pen the words that God clearly spoke to me in the middle of the night: **"From this day forward you will begin to see great change in the heart of your husband. I will begin to change and mold him into My image, a man after My own heart. He will desire the things I desire, and speak the things I would speak. Hold on to this promise for I have spoken unto you this night and surely it shall come to pass."**

I want to encourage those reading this story to be diligent in prayer. Learn to wait on the Lord and listen for His voice. Write down the things God impresses upon your heart to help affirm, confirm, and encourage you along the way, especially when it feels like your prayers are not being answered. Having a record of your promises from God will help you remember what He told you and cause your faith to soar when your promise is fulfilled.

I tucked my promise from God about my husband away in my journal and in my heart. I did not share this promise with another soul until more than a decade later.

Chapter Fourteen
The Unexpected

A year after my promise in the night, in the spring of 2003, my husband began to complain that he could not eat without feeling sick and thought he was possibly having gallbladder attacks. He became extra thin, which we attributed to long work hours, remodeling our home, and of course, not eating as much because he did not feel good after eating. On top of all this, he came home from work one evening and announced that there were rumors that the satellite clinic he had been managing for many years was going to be closed down. I encouraged him to see the doctor before we lost our health benefits.

When we went to the initial appointment, a few of his liver functions were high, causing the doctor to ask him how much he drank. Todd admitted to drinking quite a bit on a nightly basis, so the doctor recommended he cut back on his alcohol consumption. In addition, from his symptoms, she agreed that his gallbladder could be the issue, so she scheduled him the next day to have an ultrasound to check his gallbladder.

On the day of the ultrasound, I called my husband from my job at the school to ask him about the results. He had just finished the test and was on his way back to work, but he said he would know the results soon. I told him I would call him a little later, so that afternoon, during a quiet time at work, I again phoned my husband to inquire about his ultrasound results. The receptionist at his job who answered the phone informed me that Todd never returned to work after his appointment. I thought this was strange, because I knew he intended to return to work since he told me he was on his way back when I had talked to him earlier. I hung up and immediately reached my husband on his cell phone. I asked him why he never returned to work to which he responded, "I did, but I left." I immediately wanted to know why he had left work.

"I will talk to you when you get home," he responded.

I got stubborn and demanded, "No, you can talk to me now! What is going on?"

"My ultrasound report came back and they think I have cancer," he replied.

My heart stopped. I was not expecting this at all! "You're kidding, right?"

He said, "No, I'm not kidding! They see cancer in my liver."

My husband was only thirty-eight years old; we still had three kids, ages fourteen, twelve, and ten, to finish raising.

After asking to be dismissed from work for the rest of the day, I came home and cried with my husband over this unexpected news. Our minds raced with questions. What kind of cancer was it? How long had he had it? Was there more of it? He let me pray for him, and after the initial shock, I looked at him and said, "You are not going anywhere! We have three kids to raise, and you are going to help finish this job! God is able to heal you." Todd said he believed that Jesus could heal him, too.

Our life turned into continuous appointments of poking, prodding, and testing to identify the type of his cancer. A CAT scan revealed another tumor located on his thyroid, so the doctors suspected two different types of cancer; however, further testing revealed that both locations contained the same type of cancer: B-Cell Lymphoma that had already progressed to stage IV. He was immediately scheduled to see an oncologist to begin chemotherapy.

When the oncologist walked into the exam room for our first appointment, he seemed surprised by my husband's strong, healthy appearance, stating, "From your lab numbers, I expected to see a more sickly looking man." He proceeded to explain that a stem cell transplant would be used if Todd's cancer could not be put into remission or if he came out of remission at any time after treatment.

Todd started his chemotherapy treatment, and with the Lord's protection, he had minimal side effects, never missing a day of work other than for appointments. The Lord allowed Todd's body to work with the chemotherapy, and even after his very first round of treatment, Todd's ALT/AST levels dropped significantly. Todd maintained healthy blood counts and never required one blood transfusion or discontinuation of care.

I was convinced that my husband's cancer would cause him to seek the Lord for not only his healing but also for his salvation. Todd did privately seek God for his healing and also sought God publicly by asking me and others to pray. Even facing cancer, though, Todd still would not accompany me to church.

Shortly after his diagnosis, the rumor of his clinic closing was validated, and we were now faced with the possibility of losing all of our family health benefits. Through God's grace, the main lab at St. Alexius Medical Center hired my husband as a help-out employee, allowing us to maintain our income and health insurance coverage. I also sought a full-time job with benefits and was hired as a claims payer which would provide full health benefits if we should need them later.

We consulted with a team of stem cell doctors in Rochester, Minnesota at the Mayo Clinic as a precaution in case Todd was not in complete remission after his five months of chemotherapy treatment, and when the treatment finally ended, we scheduled a

PET scan to determine if he was in full remission. The night before the scan, my husband restlessly reached over, took my hand, and laid it on his chest. Not knowing what he was doing, I slid my hand back close to my side, but again, he reached for my hand and laid it on his chest. After a few moments, I slid my hand away once more. He reached for my hand a final time, laid it on his chest and said, "Tell it to be gone."

I asked, "Do you want me to pray for you?"

"Yes! Just tell it be gone," he said.

I prayed for his complete healing in Jesus' Name, remembering the evening I had prayed silently for his asthma attack in the middle of the night by laying my hand on his chest and how the Lord had healed him. The Lord used Todd's asthma to build our faith for the future obstacles that we could not see at the time.

When we received the results, Todd's PET scan was clear, indicating no cancer! God again proved Himself mighty.

Chapter Fifteen
The Return to Life as Usual

When we first received the good news of Todd's cancer being in remission, I again believed Todd would come to God. I thought maybe he had told God, "If you heal me, I will live for you and surrender my life over to you." To my disappointment, my husband quickly slipped back into his old routines and habits.

Over the course of chemotherapy treatments, Todd had given up drinking alcohol and chewing tobacco, and I hoped that the fear of recurring cancer would deter my husband from returning to his old lifestyle.

We found out Todd was in remission in August, and being an avid outdoorsman and hunter, it was just in time for hunting season. One fall afternoon, Todd and his nephew returned from a hunt and retired to the garage to clean the birds they had retrieved that day. We can access our garage through a door in our kitchen. The door has a window with vertical blinds that we normally keep shut due to the lack of scenery, but this day the blinds had been left slightly slanted. At the exact moment that I happened to glance through the window into the garage, I could see my husband being handed a tobacco can from his nephew. Without thinking twice, I pulled the door open and said, "What do you think you are doing?" They looked like two sheepish children being scolded, but I was furious that my husband seemed to already forget the mercy and grace God had shown him. My husband tried to lighten the mood with some corny remark, but I was not amused. I know I made my nephew uncomfortable because he left soon after.

By the end of that hunting season, Todd had added alcohol back into his daily routine, but he initially tried to hide it from me. Upon this discovery, I did not nag at him but did tell him, "If I were you, I would not mess with God's grace like that. You may not have it that easy next time." Although he seemed uncomfortable when I said this to him, he never got angry at me; he knew I was right. He just could not commit to letting go of his familiar lifestyle.

Our children had reached the preteen and early teen years by this time, and by God's grace and mercy, they were actively living for God and forming friendships and connections in the house of God. They were involved in the activities of the church, and for many years, they were active in both Junior and Senior Bible Quizzing at our local church.

Even though my husband silently supported our lifestyle, he could not bring himself to attend the children's activities on a regular basis. In all their years of Bible quizzing, he saw only one quiz meet when our oldest daughter was in her first year of Junior Bible Quizzing, although we invited him to all of our local meets. He came to most of their church Christmas programs but would exit as quickly as possible when they ended.

I praise God for the church family He gave us that helped me raise my children in the Truth. God connected us with some key families that took a special interest in the lives of our children, making an eternal impact. I am also thankful for every Sunday School teacher and youth leader that provided godly grounding through their leadership. Consistency and faithfulness to the house of God, mixed with prayer, created an atmosphere and opportunity for my children to become grounded and rooted in Truth.

Despite the spiritual divide evidenced in our social circles and entertainment choices, Todd and I endeavored to remain united in our efforts to correct our children when needed. He backed me in my correction, adamantly prohibiting the girls to talk disrespectfully to me. Even if I did not always agree with his correction methods, I tried not to voice my opinion in front of the children; if he grounded them, even if I thought it was unfair, I did not usurp his authority. Also, if either of us made a decision that our children did not like, we did not allow them to go ask the other parent to make the opposite decision.

Todd struggled with expressing his true feelings, causing a lack of emotional connection with his girls in their younger years. In addition to missing most of their church events, he did not share in many family-time moments or outings. He demonstrated his love by acts of service and could not hide his overprotective nature when any activity posed possible danger. He always worried about them getting hurt, even to the point that it took me some convincing just to get him to teach the girls how to mow the lawn.

I wanted my children to learn to take an active role in helping out the family and to develop responsibility and work ethic. I also knew they needed to be kept busy during summer breaks, because idleness poses a great threat to the health and spiritual direction of our young people who can easily be consumed by social media, mindless games, and instant gratification. Idleness has always been the workshop of the enemy.

"By much slothfulness the building decayeth; and through idleness of the hands the house droppeth through."
(Ecclesiastes 10:18)

In the beginning of my walk with God, Todd viewed my lifestyle and the way I tried to raise our kids as a set of rules passed down from an overbearing preacher who had too much say in our lives. However, as the years passed and our children grew, my husband's skepticism turned to pride in the direction of our daughters' lives. He did not voice his pride to them like they may have needed to hear, primarily due to his tendency to avoid situations that stirred his sentimental emotions out of fear of not knowing what to say; but, seeing the troubles of others around us as their teens began to use drugs, drink alcohol, and have behavior issues at school and home made him see the value of raising our children in a godly environment. True, we somewhat sheltered and protected our girls from most worldly activities, but they did have some exposure to the devastation and heartache a person could experience when bound by drugs, alcohol, and sin. My children had an anchor and hope in Jesus Christ. They were living epistles to their father in so many ways. He dropped his beautiful daughters off at public school and could see them stand out in their modest dress and lifestyle, and not once did they ever ask why they had to be different from the other kids at school.

Numerous times, my husband would reveal his thoughts, possibly unknowingly. He would disclose how someone he knew had a child in trouble with drugs or other issues that so many of our teens face today and would say, "I can't imagine having to go through that with our kids. I'm so glad they have their heads on straight." I would seize the moment to give the credit and glory to God, knowing that without Him, we would be in the exact same situations. I cannot thank Him enough that He saved me and opened my eyes to Truth. I remember a young man at our grocery store who went to school with our oldest daughter once said to me, "You have such nice children; I can tell you are a good mom."

I replied, "I have a good God and all the credit for any good in them is because of Him!" We definitely had some flawed parenting skills, but the Lord made up the difference.

I tried to be active in the lives of our children and made a great effort to know all of their friends both in and out of the church. I attended a seminar one time for Sunday School teachers, and the presenter, talking on raising teens, made the thought-provoking statement, "Let me spend time with your child and their friends for a few days, and I will tell you where they are spiritually." I took it to heart and carefully monitored who my children spent time with, even if they were part of our local church. I realized that just attending the same church did not make them a good influence. I was not naïve enough to think that all their friends had a desire to develop a relationship for themselves with Jesus Christ and learned that if I looked closely and watched behaviors, I could discern and identify the true nature of the heart. *"Even small children are known by their actions; so is their conduct really pure and upright?" (Proverbs 20:11, NIV)*

When our children's social circles enlarged and they became teenagers and part of our local youth group, my husband allowed me to open up our home as a place of fellowship for them to gather. We hosted birthday parties, bonfires, and all-girl pool parties. These young people significantly impacted my husband. He even allowed himself to venture out and banter and tease some of my children's closest friends, often labeling them with his own nickname as his sign of endearment. God was using these young, spirit-filled teenagers to erode the walls he lived behind.

Chapter Sixteen
Boy Meets Girl or Girl Meets Boy

The trouble with having three beautiful girls is that they eventually grow up and attract boys! Our oldest daughter, McKenzi, became smitten with Andrew, a godly, young man from our church who had been raised in a mild-mannered, godly home with a very patient father, a doting mother, and only one brother. When he decided he wanted to date McKenzi, he was thrown into the Pace village which was not as quiet and calm as his own home environment.

He already knew the Pace sisters were anything but quiet, but he faced a new level of initiation: Andrew had to face Todd Pace. He had heard all of the stories about Todd's tough exterior and that he didn't mince words, but he soon witnessed my husband's short fuse and his daily diet of drinking beer. Todd did not exude a warm and inviting aura, especially to the young man interested in one of his daughters; my husband wanted to see what Andrew was really made of before he showed any signs of approval. He made Andrew nervous, but interestingly, Andrew made Todd nervous, too. However, as time passed Andrew began to win my husband over with genuine respect and a humble spirit.

As Andrew got more serious about our daughter, to soften the blow, I privately warned my husband that Andrew and McKenzi planned on marriage in the not-so-distant future, a big deal considering McKenzi was not quite graduated from high school. Andrew was in college with plans at the time to become a mortician and possibly attend school in the state of Oregon.

87

He called me one afternoon at work and told me he wanted to propose to McKenzi on her birthday. He wanted to know what my husband's plans were for the weekend so he could invite Todd out for supper, but I told him that it would be best for him to just show up after everyone left the house that Saturday morning and ask him without any preset meeting arrangement. I said, "My husband will respect you for just being direct and not trying to win him over." I also warned him that I honestly did not know if Todd would give his consent.

Not much keeps me awake at night, but this kept me up all night praying for God's will and even for Andrew's protection. I did not know how my husband would actually react when asked this big question of marriage regarding our oldest daughter, and even if he refused to give his consent, I did not want him to become unreasonable or angry when Andrew asked him.

I spent that morning driving around our city, praying and waiting for the answer. My phone rang, and seeing my husband's number, I tried to remain calm and answer the phone in my usual manner.

My husband said, "You better come home!"

I replied, "Why? What's wrong?"

"That boy came out here today and asked if he could marry McKenzi," he responded.

My heart stopped! I exclaimed, "What did you do?!"

He started to laugh, and immediately I felt relieved! He relayed the scenario of how Andrew asked him to marry McKenzi, even bringing plastic goats and cows as a dowry, and, to my amazement, he had given his consent.

I would like to say everything sailed smoothly for the two after this, but my husband did not always cooperate while we made wedding plans. He dragged his feet on signing the marriage license for them, which was required since McKenzi would not quite be eighteen at the time of the wedding. He resisted getting to the store to get fitted for the tuxedo and grumbled about having to show up for rehearsal at the church. Todd's behavior caused dissension between McKenzi and him. Since he could not communicate to his daughter that he did not want to lose her so soon and because he felt protective of her, he acted disagreeable and negative about the upcoming wedding instead.

One evening at home, Todd commented to me about Andrew and McKenzi being so young to get married and told me some things others had said about them being too young as well. I told him that I understood the apprehension over their ages. I knew they had a lot to learn but was confident of the success of their future, because they loved God and were committed to His ways, which set them apart from many couples getting married. I also stated that I never heard anyone speaking against young people sleeping together or having babies before marriage, but when two young people who have been committed and kept themselves pure want to get married, they become the talk of the town. I stated, "I'm not ashamed that they want to do things right, and I'm confident that God will be their guide!" He never replied, but again, I believe, in his heart, he knew that they were going about this union the right way. What father who loved his daughter would not want a young man to respect and honor her, rather than take what he wants and leave her behind because he lacked commitment? Their relationship proved again to my husband that God's ways are better than our ways.

When the wedding weekend arrived in March of 2007, Todd came grudgingly to rehearsal, obviously very much out of his comfort zone. Then, the morning of the wedding, I could tell he was in a cantankerous mood, and I was his target; he couldn't show up at this Pentecostal wedding and act happy to be there, because he would have friends and relatives watching this event.

The ceremony started and a few times during the sermon, he leaned over and made snide remarks about the message. I did not react negatively but just listened quietly and let it go. On the drive over to the reception, I received a phone call informing me that my husband and his friends were in the parking lot having a tailgating party. At first, I was angry, not wanting McKenzi to arrive and see this taking place; however, I quickly got my spirit in check and prayed for God to give me grace and strength. I walked up to my husband and his friends, greeted them all politely, and went into the building. Later, Todd came to take his seat by me at dinner and whispered in my ear, "You are no fun!"

I asked, "What do you mean?"

He said, "I can't even make you mad anymore!"

"Why do you want to?" I asked.

He just chuckled in response.

During the reception, the kids presented a slide show, and my husband suddenly could not hold back his emotion. Tears began to silently fall down his cheeks, even though he fought them with all his might. When I arrived home later that evening after wedding clean up, Todd sat in our room with fresh tears of realization on his face; McKenzi would not be coming home to us.

Underneath the surface was the tender heart of a man who loved me and our children very deeply. I could see faint cracks in his exterior. God was at work!

Chapter Seventeen
More than Words on a Page

In late January of 2009, our youngest daughter, London, came bounding through my Power Hour classroom door, announcing she intended to get back into Bible Quizzing. She had not been involved for a few years and would now have to quiz on the Experienced level. The season had already started, and the first quiz meet had already taken place, so I said, "Too late."

She said, "No, Mom, please!"

I reasoned she was at least 100 verses behind and she would get burned out trying to catch up. She pleaded, and I gave in with this admonition: she had to finish what she started and had to work at it with a committed attitude. She also needed to convince someone to be her teammate, so lo and behold, she convinced her childhood friend, Daniel, to participate for a time. Eventually, a few others also sat at the buzzer so she could compete. To our surprise, London learned over 140 verses in one weekend, went to the quiz meet, and did very well. She stayed the course, digested the book of Luke, and finished the year.

Quizzing got a hold of her, and she rallied others to join her the next season for the book of Acts. We started out the next year with three Experienced quiz teams and several Intermediate teams. Ashton also joined the quizzing effort that year, even with her full schedule of college classes and a full-time job.

Over the next year, Bible Quizzing enriched my life and the lives of our children in so many ways, fostering a great spiritual impact and grounding in the lives of London and Ashton. London was a very dedicated quizzer and excelled greatly at the quiz board. One Saturday morning early on in the season, she came upstairs and shared the dream she had the night before. She explained that we were at the national Senior Bible Quizzing competition, which up to this point, we had never been involved in. She went on to tell us that she dreamt she was on stage and lined up with some other quizzers, and she was awarded Second-Highest Scoring Quizzer of the national tournament. I laughed and asked, "Why not first?"

She said, "But, Mom, it was so real! I really felt like I was there!" This, of course, became a light-hearted teasing topic throughout the year.

The quiz year ended with just London and Ashton still quizzing from our local church. We were one of two North Dakota teams headed to St. Louis, Missouri for the national competition that August. I tried to involve my husband in the girls' success by repeatedly inviting him to come watch the local meets. I would tell him all the exciting things that happened during our quiz meets and how well the girls were doing and even invited him to Nationals, but his answer always remained, "No."

The girls did not know anyone but our other ND team and a few other quizzers they had met during a quiz extravaganza in Kansas City, MO. We were all a bit nervous, not knowing what to expect out of our competition or anything else that would take place during the week. I pushed the girls to be involved and get out and meet the other quizzers, saying "We are here and we're going to make the most of it." I am so glad we did. God blessed us with lifetime friends and solidified in my heart and mind that Bible Quizzing is one of the greatest programs we have in anchoring our children in the Truth.

The other quiz families and officials made us feel right at home, and soon "the little girls from North Dakota" became a buzzword for the week. Some of the guys made a pool on what teams they thought would finish where and had put us in last place; however, when the girls started out the gate and won their first two quizzes against some pretty decent competition, those boys had to rethink their predictions. The next day, the girls had some nail-biting quizzes and lost, coming down to the last question or two. We were very pleased with how they had quizzed and were not disappointed on how things finished out.

At the end of the quiz week, we attended the awards banquet and, with surprise, accepted the Novice Team of the Year Award for the national tournament. As the ceremony moved on to recognize the top-scoring quizzers of the tournament, London's name was called as the Second-Highest Scoring Quizzer of the tournament! We should not have been surprised, because God had already revealed it to her in a dream. I tucked that away and pondered upon it over the years, realizing that it wasn't about her ability to quiz, but about God being pleased with her faithfulness to learning His Word with a sincere heart, showing her He leads and directs the steps of His children.

"The steps of a good man are ordered by the LORD: and he delighteth in his way." (Psalm 37:23)

The enemy of the soul constantly bids for the lives, time, and talents of our children. Much time and energy can be expelled by involvement in mindless activities that do not benefit our children spiritually. How much more rewarding and life changing is the activity of learning God's Word through Bible Quizzing? God's Word will forever have an impact in their lives, and even if they stray, they will never be able to get away from that powerful, living Word that they hid in their hearts and minds. God's Word will NOT return void.

"So shall my word be that goeth forth out of my mouth: it shall not return unto me void, but it shall accomplish that which I please, and it shall prosper in the thing whereto I sent it." (Isaiah 55:11)

My children have faced obstacles and temptations, and have even stumbled and fallen, but I believe God's Word has been there to pick them up and encourage them to rise again.

"Rejoice not against me, O mine enemy: when I fall, I shall arise; when I sit in darkness, the Lord shall be a light unto me." (Micah 7:8)

Chapter Eighteen
The Quiet Years

"Thou knowest how that David my father could not build an house unto the name of the LORD his God for the wars which were about him on every side, until the LORD put them under the soles of his feet. <u>But now the LORD my God hath given me rest on every side,</u> so that there is neither adversary nor evil occurrent. And, behold, I purpose to build an house unto the name of the LORD my God..." (I Kings 5:3-5, emphasis added)

These passages of scripture stood out to me one day, and I felt like the Lord showed me that after all the years of the enemy fighting against the work of God in our lives and in our home, God had given us the same rest Solomon enjoyed. Because he had a father who loved the Lord and was willing to go to battle and subdue the enemy to bring peace to his household and nation, God allowed Solomon to rest and build.

Our children were now nearly raised, and the battles between my husband and I were non-existent. Not to say we always saw eye to eye, but we now handled any disagreements between us through calm discussion.

We were also now blessed to call ourselves grandparents to a beautiful baby girl, Nicollet Michelle Sletten, born on April 28, 2009. We welcomed this new phase in our lives. Our family circle was widening and blessed, but my husband still stood on the outside of the circle spiritually.

One cannot with words alone convey the distance between a husband and a wife when they are not spiritually yoked according to God's will and design.

My daughter and son-in-law made arrangements to have Nicollet dedicated to the Lord, a momentous occasion for them as parents and for me as a grandparent. McKenzi invited her dad and her grandmothers to celebrate the day with them as they dedicated their precious firstborn to the Lord.

Dedication Sunday arrived, and I prepared to leave for church. I peeked my head out into the garage where my husband was working and asked if he would be joining us. He, to my great disappointment and disbelief, said he would not be coming. I said, "OK," shut the door between us, and stood in utter disbelief that he would refuse to come to his own granddaughter's dedication service. I couldn't understand how he continued to keep his distance. How could he not see that these little things in life were keeping him from having a close relationship with his children and now his own grandchildren?

When I arrived at the church, all the grandparents were in attendance for Nicollet's dedication except my husband. McKenzi asked if her dad was coming, and I had to tell her, "No." I watched her fight back tears of sadness and anger and knew there was nothing I could say to make it better. McKenzi and her siblings had endured their dad's absence from many memorable events in their lives, and now it looked like our grandchildren would have to endure the same.

I returned home after the service and told him how nice it was that his mom came to the dedication service and how much it meant to McKenzi. I could see the blood drain from his face as he said, "My mom came?"

I said, "Yes, and she said she really enjoyed the service. She was happy McKenzi and Andrew included her."

With those words, I left him alone in his garage to think. I knew I need not say anything else, because I could tell Todd recognized that he had again made the wrong decision and again had to live with regret. I prayed and asked God to deal with him and to somehow comfort McKenzi and her sisters and heal them from the hurt and disappointments they had suffered.

98

Chapter Nineteen
Losses and Gains

"Lo, children are an heritage of the LORD and the fruit of the womb is his reward. As arrows are in the hand of a mighty man; so are children of the youth. Happy is the man that hath his quiver full of them: they shall not be ashamed, but they shall speak with the enemies in the gate." (Psalm 127:3-5)

McKenzi and Andrew announced in the spring of 2010 that we would be blessed again with a grandchild that November. We all rejoiced over the exciting news! We already thought Nicollet was a great blessing and could not wait to add another.

Since Andrew could not attend McKenzi's first obstetric appointment to check for the baby's heartbeat, she asked me to go with her. I remember feeling a bit uneasy or unsettled when we arrived at the doctor's office, and when they brought us into the exam room and began to listen for the baby's heartbeat, they could not get a sound on the Doppler. I started praying silently, and I could see the look of concern on McKenzi's face when they called the doctor in, who promptly ordered an ultrasound. I stayed in the waiting room, praying, until McKenzi came out, and thankfully, they found our precious grandchild and everything appeared fine.

Months passed and McKenzi began to look like she was expecting again. We celebrated the Fourth of July holiday and made our way to the annual family church camp, but in one service at camp, I noticed that McKenzi seemed preoccupied or distant. The Lord often allows me to notice these things and nudges me, but I do not always respond out of fear that I am off base or reading more deeply into something than I should. During the night, McKenzi had an asthma attack and just didn't seem to be feeling all that great.

We came home from camp, and McKenzi and Andrew went to the clinic without telling any of us that she had not felt the baby move for several days. The ultrasound confirmed their fears: their precious unborn baby was no longer living.

My husband, when he heard the news, left his job for the day and made his way to Andrew and McKenzi's home, arriving before me. He watched as they leaned on God through the devastation of losing this eagerly awaited baby before ever getting to meet her.

McKenzi delivered their precious angel baby, Bristol Elizabeth, on July 15, 2010, and they laid their little girl to rest on July 16, 2010. This beautiful, godly, young couple had to trust that all things work together for the good and say, *"...the LORD gave, and the LORD hath taken away: blessed be the name of the LORD." (Job 1:21)*

We cannot always understand why painful things happen, but we can know that God will strengthen and comfort us. I have seen great spiritual growth in the lives of McKenzi and her husband since that time. They remained faithful, and God is using them in ministry as youth pastors in our local church.

A short six months after we buried Bristol, right before our Sunday morning service began, I felt like McKenzi was expecting again. When I asked her, she said, "How do you always know?" and confirmed that she was eight and a half weeks along.

Andrew was scheduled to preach that morning and before the service, he told McKenzi that he felt like God wanted him to announce to the church that they were expecting again and that

God had told him not to fear. She agreed he should follow God's prompting, so he stepped out in faith, not allowing fear to steal the joy of this new blessing. On August 15, 2011, we were again blessed with a beautiful granddaughter, Jordin Sara Sletten.

The Lord has not promised us a life without heartache or pain, but He has promised that He would never leave or forsake us.

The image of our children laying their child to rest forever in the arms of the Lord before getting to know her or raise her will forever be etched in my mind. As a grandmother, I often wonder how she would look and act if she was with us today. I can't imagine how much more her parents think about this precious child, yet through it all, I have seen them let the Healer of their broken hearts keep them and mend them.

Chapter Twenty
Entering a New Season of Life

My husband and I moved Ashton to Indianapolis to attend Indiana Bible College that same August of 2011.

My life took on a new dimension, transitioning from the demanding schedule of child rearing and attending my children's events to a less restricted schedule. I watched the Lord work and move in the lives of my children, and with excitement, I dreamed of how God could use them for His service. However, I also wondered what would happen in my own life without the constant purpose of raising my children and training them to love and live for the Lord. I continued to pray for them to be instruments in the kingdom of God, but I knew they must now live for Him independently from me. I often thought about what would happen to my marriage as our children exited our home to make homes of their own.

Todd and I ran very independently from one another on a social level. Todd came and went from our home without opposition from me, spending nearly every Friday night after work with his brother at the bar. On Saturdays, he either worked around our yard and home or went hunting, fishing, or golfing. I came and went on the weekends with errands or church activities.

We did often get together on Saturday evenings as a family, and we would have McKenzi, Andrew, and our grandkids out for supper. However, beyond that, our commonality was deeply rooted in our children. Even though Todd was not as actively involved in their activities, I tried to communicate to him what they were doing and would look to him for advice or permission for the things they needed.

During this time of transition, I sensed a new type of sadness or loneliness in my husband. He often seemed down and made comments on how unhappy he was with life in general. Looking from the outside, you would have to ask yourself, "Why?" He had a decent-paying job, a sensible home with a beautiful three-acre yard, a boat, a camper, and plenty of hunting and fishing equipment. Additionally, he had friends he went out with; his children were living decent, productive lives, and he had grandchildren! How could he not see all the good in his life and feel happy and blessed?

I knew he felt left out of our lives, even though he always refused when we tried to invite or include him in our activities. When the kids came home to visit with the grandkids or when we had holiday gatherings, he would eat with us, make some small talk, and then hide himself away in the garage or hole up in our master bedroom.

He seemed incapable of breaking out of his routine of self-isolation. Each evening, he came home, changed clothes, popped open his can of beer, did some chores, and proceeded to drink alone in his garage until bedtime.

I often tried to gently point out to him all the blessings in his life, but I knew that no matter what he added to his life, good or bad, it would never be enough. He had an aching and void in his life that only God could fill. So, I watched helplessly as my husband battled against his discontentment in the only way he knew: one beer at a time.

By the summer of 2013, my husband's moods became increasingly sad. Most who knew him would not have recognized the change, because he was a master at concealing the turmoil within. However, when we were alone, I could feel, and almost see, the cloud of sadness hanging over him.

One evening, my sister and mother stopped in to see us while my husband was in one of his antagonistic moods. I tried to gloss over his mood so my mother and sister would not notice, but at one point in the conversation, he made a comment over something he heard, and I felt a sharp ugliness coming from his remark. I changed the subject and the conversation moved on, but I silently ached for him and his unhappiness.

That evening in prayer, I talked to the Lord about what I was seeing and feeling, saying, "Lord, something has to change; he is more unhappy every day! He hates life, while being surrounded with blessings! He chooses to separate himself from us during family activities and then feels as if we have alienated him."

I was so bothered by what had happened the night before that I even shared what I was seeing with a close friend, telling her, "He is living a lonely, miserable existence right in the middle of what so many people wish they had: great kids, beautiful grandchildren, and healing from stage IV cancer! Yet, he is still miserable!"

I also told the Lord, "I am tired of feeling like I have to tiptoe around him because he is so moody! I'm tired of trying to function as a family and make family memories that are not fully shared by him." I grieved over all the years my children did things without his presence, and though they loved him in spite of it all, I knew time could not be turned back. I pleaded, "Please, Lord! It has been so long!"

Ashton, London, and I left early that August to catch the tail end of National Bible Quizzing and attend Youth Congress in Louisville, Kentucky before leaving London in Indianapolis for a second year at Indiana Bible College. We had a great conference, especially since McKenzi and her husband surprised us by driving through the night to meet us on the first night of Youth Congress.

We returned home on August 12, 2013. While we were gone, my husband spent the weekend drinking heavily with friends.

Exactly one week later, on Monday evening, August 19, 2013, my kids and I were at my mom's house for what we refer to as "Grandma Betty Night." Before I went to her house, I spoke with my husband on the phone around five o'clock in the evening, as he routinely called to ask if I had any special orders to which he knew I usually responded, "No." He mentioned he needed to work in the garden, and we hung up.

After supper at Grandma Betty's, we usually went to the church for family prayer night, but Ashton asked if she could be excused to go home because of all the long hours she had been working. I agreed she could go home and took off for the church, but when I reached the door to the basement stairwell of our church to head up for prayer, my phone started to ring. Glancing down, I noticed Ashton's number, so I stopped and answered. She immediately exclaimed, "There is something wrong with Dad! You have to come home!"

When I asked what was going on, she started to cry and said, "I don't know! I found him on the floor!"

I quickly replied, "OK, I will be right there."

I stopped my son-in-law as he came in and told him, "Have the church pray. Ashton found Todd on the floor!"

I called "911" from my car and learned that Ashton had already called; help was on the way. As I drove, I prayed and felt God bring a calm to my spirit. I said aloud, "I don't know what is happening, and I don't know how bad it might be, but I know that You are going to save him! You will not let him leave this earth without being saved first." I knew God had made me a promise, and He was going to fulfill it!

When I arrived home, Ashton had been able to get him up from the floor and had him seated at our kitchen table with his head lying down. His skin was clammy; his eyes were bewildered, and his speech was slurred. I thought maybe he had a stroke or a heart attack, so when he looked up when I entered, I made him lay his head back down. I held his hand and prayed for God's protection, reassuring him that everything was going to be ok. Just as I finished praying, the ambulance arrived, and the paramedics quickly loaded him up and headed for the emergency room.

When I arrived at the hospital, the ambulance personnel reported that, while loading Todd into the ambulance, he had a Grand Mal seizure. My husband had never had an epileptic seizure before in his life.

I notified Todd's mom, a registered nurse who works for a local neurologist in our city. She called the doctor she worked for, who immediately came to the hospital to help with Todd's care. He had labs run on my husband, and the results came back with several elevated numbers. The doctor came to my husband's bedside and asked him if he drank a lot. I nodded my head affirmatively, and my husband agreed. The doctor was concerned that Todd had a seizure out of the blue with no prior history and about some other numbers that could affect his kidneys.

He looked my husband in the eye and said, "You and I are going to have a serious talk!" He proceeded to tell my husband that he needed to stop his excessive drinking and talked to him about some of the labs and the need to order a CAT scan. My husband's creatinine level was high, and the team worried about a pulmonary embolism. The doctor decided to admit my husband for observation and an MRI, since the staff was positive that he had not had a heart attack or a stroke. My husband kept complaining that the muscles in his chest were extra sore.

The next morning, the MRI images revealed a right parietal lobe brain tumor. His neurologist believed it was in an operable location, and from the images and the way it was shaped, he suspected the tumor was benign. However, my husband's creatinine level became a great concern, being way above the normal range, so the doctor arranged for Todd to be flown immediately to Rochester, Minnesota to receive consultation and possible surgery to remove the tumor at Mayo Clinic.

With very little time to think, I raced home to throw a few items in a suitcase while my mother-in-law flew with my husband to Rochester. I knew the drive would be way too long for her on her own, and I needed time to gather a few things. My dear friend, Laurie, insisted on coming with me to help drive and to assist me if needed, and I was so thankful to have her come, even though I knew it tore her away from her own family.

We arrived in Rochester at about three o'clock in the morning and slept a few hours before heading to St. Mary's hospital where my husband had been admitted. When we arrived at the hospital, my husband's kidney functions were still on the rise, and the pain in his body was getting out of control. He had developed a condition from the violent seizures he had the day before called Rhabdomyolysis, which caused his muscles to break down and release lactic acid so quickly that his kidneys could not keep up. He underwent more scans and thorough examinations, including a spinal tap to rule out a return of Lymphoma that possibly had settled in his brain. The PET scan revealed there was no other cancer located in his body.

Due to my husband's kidney crisis, the brain tumor surgery had to be postponed while they battled to keep Todd from going into kidney failure. Finally, after many days, Todd's creatinine level began to drop; however, he still had horrible discomfort from the muscle pain in his body.

The neurosurgeon met with us, feeling it was best to send Todd back home to heal and to return in September for a resection of the tumor. He assured us that it looked very much like a benign brain tumor that was in an accessible spot for removal.

About a month later, on September 16, 2013, we returned to Rochester for another MRI and placement of markers for the brain mapping they would use for guides during the surgery. The doctor warned us of the slight possibility of partial paralysis or permanent left-sided weakness from the procedure.

The next morning, they prepared my husband for surgery and just before taking him away, our children, Todd's mother, and I had the opportunity to pray with him.

After many long hours of surgery, Todd was in recovery, and the nurse communicator called for me to come meet with the neurosurgeon. I took my mother-in-law with me to meet with the doctor, and he came in and informed us that he got most of the tumor but not all. He explained that when he got too close to the motor area, it caused Todd to have a seizure, so he knew it would be too risky to continue, clarifying that they always strive for quality of life in these situations. He reiterated, to our relief, that he felt the tumor was benign but that the final diagnosis of the tumor would be determined over the next week by pathology.

Todd was awake and alert when they brought him to the ICU, and the very next day, he was up walking around and was released to a neurosurgical floor. After only two days, he was released to come home, as strong as he had always been but just needing to allow himself time to recover before returning to work.

Because of his very brief stay in the hospital, the pathology reports were not complete when Todd was released.

The Sunday after returning home from Rochester, I asked my husband if he would like to come to church with me, and he replied, "Thanks, but I think I will pass".

I said, "OK," and once again, went to church without him.

Chapter Twenty-One
The Game Changer

On Monday, September 23, 2014, my husband received a phone call from his neurosurgeon, Dr. Jacobs, and as I observed the conversation from the doorway, I could see the color leave my husband's face and could hear a controlled, anxious quiver enter his voice. The doctor apologized repeatedly, because what he had presumed was a benign tumor now had a diagnosis of a malignant brain tumor, glioblastoma grade IV, the monster of all brain tumors. This aggressive, infiltrative tumor trenches its way into the brain tissue and, even after resection, leaves microscopic tentacles planted that eventually recur as another tumor. The median life expectancy for most of the patients with this diagnosis is fourteen to sixteen months, even with surgery, radiation, and chemotherapy treatment.

We now faced the task of breaking the news to our children, family, and friends.

Todd wanted me to make the calls, so I began with our daughters one by one. I asked all of them to pray for his healing, and above all else, for his salvation.

London was still in Indianapolis attending Bible College, and the news caused her a wave of fear and heartache. I am thankful for the students and ministers who covered her in prayer.

Ashton arrived home from work that day, and I had to tell her of her dad's bad news. As she struggled with the news and began to fall apart, I looked her in the eye and said, "We have been praying for him for over 20 years! We must now believe, more than ever, that he will allow God to save him, and that this is all part of His plan!"

Ashton replied, "But, I don't want him to die!"

I said, "He may not die, because God can heal him, but if he does die, I do not want him to be lost! The greatest miracle of all is still salvation!"

"The Lord is not slack concerning his promise, as some men count slackness; but is longsuffering to us-ward, not willing that any should perish, but that all should come to repentance." (II Peter 3:9)

A few days before we found out about Todd's brain tumor diagnosis, we learned that Brother and Sister Harrod, missionaries to Spain, would be in our church for service that coming Friday night. They were in the United States on deputation and were holding healing services throughout North Dakota. Due to their great faith, the Harrods had seen God perform many miracles around the country. I went to the garage that evening where Todd was tinkering, and I told him, "On Friday, we have a missionary coming through, and I hear he has been seeing many miracles take place. We are having a special healing service, and YOU are coming with us to church on Friday."

He looked at me and said, "OK."

I was excited and told others from the church to be praying! We bound together, believing for his healing and salvation.

The expectancy that my husband would fully surrender and get baptized that evening was so high that some of the people from our church family paid to fly our youngest daughter home to surprise my husband. They did not want her to be left out.

London arrived home on Thursday, and my husband was in our room sleeping when she came in. We all sat quietly sitting in our living room, waiting for him to wake up. When he finally came into the living room and laid eyes on our youngest daughter sitting on the couch, he was overcome with emotion and began to weep. He sat next to her, hugging her, and crying. I will never forget that moment.

The next evening, for the first time in our history, we made our way to church as a family. Brother Harrod preached a powerful message on faith and miracles, and at the close of his message, he implored the church to step out in faith and come forward for healing. I pulled my husband to the front of the church, and we began to pray. My husband participated but kept his eyes open the entire time; he looked like a scared little boy and would not let me get more than a few inches away from him. God was moving on him and you could tell he was not sure what to do about it.

Though not the landslide salvation experience we had been expecting, this night marked the beginning of the journey on the road of God's abundant mercy and grace.

Chapter Twenty-Two
The Journey Begins

Todd began to regularly attend Sunday afternoon worship services with us. In the beginning, he would not raise his hands freely and only rarely participated in singing. The whole environment was foreign territory for him.

Todd encountered a few bumps in the road as conviction set in, actually walking out of several sermons because he did not want to hear the message. Once, Pastor Michael Chuppe (my former coworker who was now my pastor) came and apologized to me when he saw Todd get up and walk out, but I told my pastor that he needed to continue to preach the Word and that he had no reason to apologize. I knew that for Todd to make it, I just had to get out of the way and let the Lord continue to fight the battle for his soul, so I never said a word to my husband after the services he exited early. I decided that the Lord could handle him better than I ever could, and I wanted to make sure that I did not hinder God's plan by trying to set my husband straight. I just needed to be still.

"And Moses said unto the people, Fear ye not, <u>stand still, and see the salvation of the LORD</u>, which he will shew you today: for the Egyptians whom ye have seen today, ye shall see them again no more for ever." (Exodus 14:13, emphasis added)

"Ye shall not need to fight in this battle: set yourselves, <u>stand ye still, and see the salvation of the LORD</u> with you, O

Judah and Jerusalem fear not, nor be dismayed; tomorrow go out to face them, for the LORD is with you." (II Chronicles 20:17, emphasis added)

If my memory has not failed me, I believe Todd stayed away from one or two services after each perceived offense, but he always returned. We never discussed the details of why he was offended, but I was always happy when he worked through it on his own.

Todd endured several weeks of radiation and chemotherapy and was given a four week break in December of 2013. After the break, he would have to begin six more months of chemotherapy to attack his brain tumor.

For Christmas of 2013, our children ordered and engraved a King James, Thompson Chain Bible for their dad. My husband began reading his Bible daily, and God began to reveal Truth to him as he read and absorbed God's Word. Periodically, he would tell me of something he learned, and I remember one afternoon, he said, "It's not right to tattoo your body!"

I said, "I agree, who told you that?"

He replied, "I was reading about it in the Bible."

"Ye shall not make any cuttings in your flesh for the dead, nor print any marks upon you: I am the LORD." (Leviticus 19:28)

In January of 2014, Todd agreed to attend Indiana Bible College's live choir recording where our youngest daughter would be singing in the chorale, a select group of singers in the choir. I almost had to pinch myself when he agreed to travel with me to see this event.

116

Calvary Tabernacle in Indianapolis, Indiana was packed the night of IBC's live recording; we arrived early to obtain decent seats where we could view our daughter in the chorale. The concert was not just a performance but a night of worship, and by the last song, God's spirit filled the chapel. Todd clapped unto the Lord and raised his hands above his head throughout the entire concert. He had finally reached a place of surrender and freedom to worship.

I could feel the Holy Ghost so strong and asked God to fill my husband with the Holy Ghost. From across the aisle, a young man from the college came and laid his hands on my husband, and I could tell Todd was being touched in a powerful way by the Holy Ghost. When he finally sat down, I looked at him and asked, "Did you get the Holy Ghost?"

He nodded his head affirmatively, but then he shrugged and said, "I don't know."

I knew my limits and backed off, not wanting to press him any further on the subject.

We returned home, and over the next six months, Todd continued his chemotherapy regimen with MRI's every few months. He again went through a valley of depression and still refused to submit to the salvation message of water baptism in Jesus' Name. He also still did not claim to have received the baptism of the Holy Ghost. Meanwhile, all of Todd's MRI's kept coming back with good reports, and we praised God for each one!

On Mother's Day, May 11, 2014, our pastor closed his powerful message on water baptism and the significance of using the name of Jesus in baptism. *"Neither is there salvation in any other: for there is none other name under heaven given among men, whereby we must be saved." (Acts 4:12)* As the Holy Ghost began to sweep through the congregation, many people came to the altar, six people were baptized in Jesus' name, and several received the Holy Ghost. My husband wept as he watched how God moved on each person, and he worshipped and thanked God for what was taking place, yet he did not make a move to be baptized.

One of the saints in the church came and asked me if she could speak to my husband, as she felt heavily burdened for him. I asked him if he would listen to what she had to say, and when he agreed, she spoke in love and implored my husband to make a decision for his soul. She said, "Sir, I beg you to make a decision. Give your children peace, knowing that if something happens to you, they will see you again." My husband received it well, and even gave her a small hug, telling her, "I am in the decision-making process."

Todd finished his chemotherapy rounds June 1, 2014 and would now just return for routine checks once a month and a follow up MRI every two months. He felt fairly strong and even began jogging again to get back into shape.

On July 1, 2014, we celebrated 26 years of marriage! God had blessed us with three children, one son-in-law, and three beautiful grandchildren with another on the way!

Later that month, the time for our annual church camp arrived, but I was unable to attend the whole week. My daughters and a couple of their friends planned a road trip to attend one of the evening services of our annual church camp on Tuesday, July 8, and, since the camp is several hours away from where we live, I joined them in one vehicle to enjoy visiting and listening to praise music along the way.

Just as we turned onto the gravel road pointing us toward the campground, my phone began to ring. I did not recognize the phone number, so I decided not to answer it, but just a few seconds later, I received a text message from my husband's nephew, Brenton, telling me that a neighbor he personally knew found Todd in a ditch near our home. They took him by ambulance to the emergency room. I immediately returned to Bismarck, and on the way back, my husband phoned me from the hospital and said that he was doing fine. He told me that as he neared home during his jog, he felt a strange tingling in his left hand and recognized that feeling from months before when he had his initial seizure. He sat down in the ditch to see if the feeling would pass and to get his cell phone ready in case he needed to call for help and said he could remember the seizure taking hold.

The next day, my husband was down and upset over having had the seizure. I also learned that Todd had weaned himself off of his seizure medication months prior, because he knew the medication contributed to the depression and foul moods he was experiencing. His neurologist made adjustments to his seizure meds to help alleviate some of these negative side effects, but Todd was once again put on a six-month probation from driving due his Grand Mal seizure. I, once again, was enlisted to be his chauffeur!

I asked him that morning why he had not yet made a decision to be baptized in Jesus' name. He answered, "I've already been baptized," referring to his infant baptism. I urged him to study the book of Acts for himself, but I knew Todd already understood the salvation message as he had been hearing the preached plan of salvation now for over nine months.

He then replied, "I will do it, if you really want me to."

I said, "That's not how it works! You need to do it for yourself." I continued, "It's your personal walk with God. I already have my own!"

At the end of the week, Todd came with me to camp to listen to Bro. Paul Mooney preach. During this powerful service, Todd and I went to the front, and the Holy Ghost again moved mightily.

That following Sunday, July 13, 2014, my husband was baptized in the beautiful, saving name of Jesus Christ. All his sins were washed away! When he came back to our pew afterwards, I asked again, "Did you receive the Holy Ghost?"

He looked at me and said "I already got it."

"When?" I replied.

He said, "Well, I got it when we went to London's live recording in January," but he indicated that he had wanted it to happen again before he said anything. God had fulfilled his promise!

All the years of praying and waiting now seemed like a brief moment in time!

Chapter Twenty-Three
The Journey Continues

When my husband was initially taken to Mayo Clinic at the very beginning of his illness, I was reading the Word, and a scripture about God revealing the *secret* things unto his people really stuck out to me. ***"The LORD confides in those who fear him; he makes his covenant known to them." (Psalm 25:14, NIV)*** The Lord had been with us every step of the way and was gently speaking into our lives.

On September 5, 2014, I sat, waiting on the Lord after my morning prayer time, and felt God speak to me in a gentle, quiet voice. **"You are My child; I love you. I will hide you in the cleft of the rock. Remember when storms gather in that I am still with you. I am your anchor."**

I replied, "Whatever lies ahead, God, give me strength. Help me to come out as pure gold. I cannot do it on my own."

At that moment in time, everything seemed to be moving in the right direction: Todd was feeling good and working full-time, and his prior MRI's were showing no new evidence of tumor recurrence.

On September 8, 2014, I again felt like God spoke to me, and I wrote as I felt God speak, **"I will begin to move you away from the shore. Do not be afraid. If you learn to let go, I will teach you to swim above the waves. Begin to fast."** I asked the Lord to be formed in me. As much as I desired to move out deeper, I had to admit that it scared me, so I asked the Lord to remove doubt and fear and to help me get past hindrances that take me back to the shore. I obeyed and began to fast as I felt led by God's spirit.

On Monday, September 15, 2014, I again felt like the Lord gave me a scripture which I will reveal later. I stared at the verse for a long time and thought, "Lord, are you showing me and preparing me or am I just reading into it because of my situation?"

This also happened to be the day that Todd and I would return to the doctor's office to go over the MRI he had before the weekend. We waited in the doctor's office, hoping to hear once again that his MRI revealed no new tumor activity; however, much to our dismay, the doctor told us that there was a change on the MRI, and it looked like tumor progression. She advised Todd to return to Mayo Clinic to consult with a neurosurgeon for another resection if possible. He also faced more chemotherapy and a good possibility of more radiation.

Todd and I attended revival services with Bro. Wayne Huntley at our local church before returning to Mayo Clinic, and my husband was touched by the Holy Ghost. On our way home that evening, he began sharing some of the things he was seeing in the Word of God, and sometimes, I had to blink twice to make sure this was actually my husband speaking. He said, "It's so cool how sometimes you think about something in the Bible, and then they preach on it!"

Todd grew spiritually after the news of his tumor progression; he prayed, read his Bible, and trusted that God had it all in His hands. Even though we could not see the future, we had peace.

On September 25, 2014, I wrote concerning our situation, "After twenty-four years of prayer and waiting, I cannot feel down about being able to walk through the doors of church on a Sunday morning with my husband at my side. To be able to raise our hands in unity to the Lord who gives us life...To be able to talk of God's great love and mercy without opposition... How can I not say thanks in all things concerning us?"

"And we know that all things work together for good to them that love God, to them who are the called according to his purpose." (Romans 8:28)

Todd was scheduled to have another surgery to remove as much of the tumor as they could on September 30, 2014. In the middle of the night, since neither of us could sleep, we sat up talking, and I asked Todd if he was alright.

He answered, "I'm worried about the kids."

Unsure of his meaning, I said, "Well, they are all big now." He asked if I was worried, and I answered, "Not as scared as the first time." When he inquired about the difference, I replied, "Because this time, I know if something happens to you, you are ready to go."

He affirmed that this assurance definitely made things better this time around, but he still seemed unsettled, wanting to see the kids before the surgery just in case something went wrong. He asked if I thought the kids would be awake soon, so we could Facetime them before he checked into the hospital at 5:30 a.m. At about 7:00 a.m. we used Facetime to visit with our kids.

Todd was first on the surgery schedule, was in the operating room a much shorter time than expected, and only spent fifteen minutes in the recovery area. When he got out of the recovery room, he asked the nurse to come get me. When I got to his room, he immediately said, "Go get the kids." He wanted them all, even the grandkids.

When they walked through the door, he was moved with emotion. He looked at McKenzi and asked her to hold his hand.

This small gesture would appear insignificant to most, but to our family, we recognized the miracle. McKenzi, as the oldest, was exposed to more of her father's anger and did not have this kind of relationship with him, but God was repairing breaches. My husband had always loved our children and provided for them, but now he began to express his love on a level they had never experienced before. He looked at our son-in-law, Andrew, and told him to keep preaching the Word and spreading the Gospel.

Later, when we were alone, he asked me to come and pray with him. We thanked Jesus for bringing Todd through another surgery without any deficits, and miraculously, just a few short hours after surgery, my husband got out of bed and walked around the ICU department.

Todd was released from the hospital just a few days after his surgery and we returned home. He started a new regimen of radiation and chemotherapy but returned to work without any restrictions.

The year came to a close, and we looked with hope and confidence as we entered the New Year of 2015. I was feeling a deep drawing to prayer and searching after God for His will, and I also felt like the Lord was dealing with me again about writing this book. I had felt impressed several times over a span of years that God wanted me to write a book, but the subject always remained unclear, especially because my husband was not anywhere near salvation when God first started nudging me.

We received a good report in February of 2015: Todd's MRI looked fantastic! The doctor said, "Go and enjoy your life!" Todd really believed God had healed him.

On Sunday, February 15, 2015, the Lord filled our oldest grandchild, Nicollet, with the baptism of the Holy Ghost. What a privilege to pray with her and witness her receive God's promise.

The grandfather who refused to attend her dedication got to witness her receive the baptism of the Holy Ghost. He was also there when she was baptized in the wonderful, saving name of Jesus on March 1, 2015. We dedicated our youngest granddaughter to the Lord on the same day, and eleven members of Todd's family attended the service. As they watched, Todd worshipped Jesus, unashamed of the One who saved him by His grace! He even stepped out and prayed with his nephew, David.

I stood in awe as these events unfolded. I believe I told my oldest daughter or one of my friends that I wished I could express the MAGNITUDE of the MIRACLE that had occurred in our lives!

A few weeks later, I received a phone call from Sister Lori Simons, the North Dakota District Ladies' Ministry president, asking me if I would be willing to be the afternoon speaker for our Ladies' Conference in May. I was shocked, humbled, and just a tad bit nervous, but I agreed. She wanted me to share my testimony of what God had done in our lives. When I hung up, I felt God's presence and wept and thanked Him for giving me a testimony of grace and mercy.

On April 2, 2015, my husband turned 50! We celebrated with joy! I never thought someone would be so excited to turn 50, but after all Todd had been through, we were thankful to still have him with us.

126

Chapter Twenty-Four
The Return

On Sunday, May 3, 2015, right after our Ladies' Conference, my husband experienced several small focal seizures during our church service. I called for our pastor and my son-in-law to pray for him at the back of the church. The seizures subsided, and he seemed to be alright.

Four days later, I wrote that Todd felt some numbness intermittently in some of his fingers in his left hand, and I was concerned he was having a recurrence. At the end of my prayer time that day, I felt in my spirit, **"Time is approaching fast. I will be near."** I wasn't sure if the Lord was referring to His soon return or preparing me for something with my husband.

On Sunday, May 10, 2015, God moved into our local church service and spoke through tongues and interpretation, saying, **"I have filled this place with My presence, and in My name, I can tear down strongholds and every evil and wicked imagination. I am able to deliver. Ask of Me and I will answer."**

That same service, my friend Amanda came and prayed for Todd and me. She spoke what God had laid on her heart for us, simply stating, **"What God has completed cannot be undone."** Todd and I once again claimed his physical healing.

On May 13, 2015, I again felt God speak to me as I waited in His presence at the end of my prayer time. He said, **"Write your story. It is about to unfold. You must be ready. Be faithful. Pray!"**

May of 2015 seemed to be a monumental month of God dealing with and revealing things to me. I often go back to that month to remind myself to refocus and push forward in God.

For the Memorial Day weekend, Todd and I escaped to beautiful Yellowstone National Park, immersing ourselves in all the wonders of our Creator. It was a special and memorable trip for both of us.

June approached, and I realized that every morning, Todd asked me to button his sleeve on the right side. At first I didn't question it but just reached out and mechanically helped him before he went off to work; however, after several mornings, it dawned on me that something must be wrong. I called him and asked if he was having trouble with his left hand, and in typical Todd fashion, he responded, "Maybe." I became a little more direct, and he admitted it was difficult to button the small buttons. In just a few short weeks, he was no longer able to even tie his ties.

On Wednesday, June 17th, Todd had a significant increase in numbness to his left hand and arm, along with numbness on the left side of his face. His lip and eyelid developed a small twitch-like movement. The next morning, I reported Todd's symptoms to his oncologist who believed these symptoms evidenced an active recurrence, so we were told we needed to return to Rochester to consult with the doctors at Mayo Clinic as soon as possible. He helped us arrange a Neuro-Oncology consult and an MRI for Monday, June 29, 2015.

Todd was in good spirits, even with the newly developed symptoms, and continued to believe that God had healed him. I was feeling a little down about the possibility of spending another summer away from home and uneasy about what was ahead of us. I mentioned one morning that it seemed we just couldn't get a break, and my husband stopped me and said, "We have received a lot of breaks!"

I knew exactly what he meant. We both knew how good the Lord had been to us, even though we did not deserve it. Our blessings far outweighed anything we were going through.

His new MRI confirmed tumor progression with radiation necrosis. He also had a significant amount of brain swelling. They talked to us about switching to a chemotherapy called Avastin, and Todd, evidently already having researched this process, replied, "Is there anything else I can try? We both know Avastin won't help get rid of the tumor; it will just slow it down for a while."

We inquired about the polio vaccine that some GBM patients were receiving on a trial at Duke University, but the Mayo doctors told us they had a similar trial, except they used the measles virus. We agreed to stay a few extra days to meet with the trial team.

During our downtime, we decided to get away from Rochester, the city that only reminded us of sickness, hospital stays, and MRIs. We drove to LaCrosse, Wisconsin, and the Lord blessed us with a reasonable deal at a hotel located on the riverfront. That evening in the hotel, I felt the weight of the world hanging on me and knew I needed to escape and be alone with God. I had a moment of fear as I considered the risks of another surgery and of participating in the experimental treatment, but right while I felt surrounded by this heaviness, I received reassurance from a friend back home that we were being covered in prayer.

Todd was so determined to do things on his own with his left hand, but buckling and zipping his own pants became a huge challenge for him. It hurt to watch this active, strong, coordinated man struggle with the simple activities of daily living.

We spent our 27th wedding anniversary, July 1, 2015, at doctors' appointments, then drove back home with instructions to return by July 9th to begin Todd's measles trial for his brain tumor.

"And they that know thy name will put their trust in thee: for thou, LORD, hast not forsaken them that seek thee."
(Psalm 9:10)

Before I ever knew about Todd's tumor progression, I had prayed a specific prayer over our finances due to our increased medical expenses from treatment and travelling to and from Rochester. I asked God for a certain amount of money, promising to return half of the amount back to His kingdom. God provided *more* than what I asked, and I kept my promise!

Additionally, our youngest daughter, about to enter her last year of Bible College, struggled with how she would return to school because of lack of funds. Todd and I were not in a financial position to pay for her tuition, but as we sat in the clinic waiting room discussing how London could possibly go back and finish school, we received a text message from a saint in the church who said they felt like they should help with London's tuition. Todd and I could not believe our eyes! God is always on time.

We discovered later that, during that time, our youngest daughter was attending our district family camp and had told the Lord that if it was His will for her to return to IBC, she needed a certain dollar amount to get back. God met her need! He is a prayer answering God, and we can put our trust in Him and in His timing.

On Friday, July 10, 2015, a round of measles virus was injected into the location of the tumor in Todd's brain. Although it was an outpatient procedure, we had to return to the clinic daily for blood work and other labs to monitor the level of the virus he had received. Todd seemed to tolerate the procedure well and was scheduled to have his tumor resection and second round of the virus inserted on Tuesday, July 14, 2015.

With lots of time on our hands, we found the Pentecostal church of Rochester, pastored by Bro. Kaske, and we attended that Sunday. They received us warmly and during the morning service, Bro. Kaske taught on the seasons of life. The night before, I had been writing about the same subject and after service, Todd said he had been reading along the same vein of thought in the book of Deuteronomy. I enjoyed watching my husband study God's Word.

Bro. Kaske referred to a verse in Amos that says, "*...prepare to meet thy God." (Amos 4:12)* Todd never talked of not making it, because he had great faith in God to heal him, and he never wanted to allow doubt to cloud his mind. I, too, struggled because I wanted to believe. We already knew God had healed him of stage IV lymphoma before, so this tumor was not a bigger problem for God. NOTHING is too hard for God.

Todd's mom and our children arrived the Monday evening before Todd's surgery, and he spent most of Tuesday morning in the operating room, this surgery seemingly taking longer than the last time. I finally received a call from the nurse communicator who stated they were having difficulty waking him, definitely not what we hoped to hear. Time passed slowly in the waiting room as the family apprehensively waited to hear more news, until finally, I received the call that Todd was awake and the doctor wanted to meet with me.

I ushered my mother-in-law and daughters to the operating room waiting area where Dr. Parney met us and informed us that Todd currently could not move his left side. They had taken him to do a CT scan to make sure he did not have any unusual bleeding going on, which, thankfully, he did not. The surgeon continued that Todd had started moving his left leg a bit and the left side of his face was responding better, but he was still unable to move his left arm. He thought that perhaps overnight more movement would return but could make no promises. Todd had been optimistic that surgery would restore some of the loss he already had in his left hand. I shuddered to think of the frustration he must be feeling with this development.

When I saw him a short while later, he was suffering with pain caused by a corneal abrasion he had received during surgery. His pain lasted through the night and, unable to sleep in the midst of excruciating pain, he said he had a song on his mind. I asked him which one, and he groggily replied, "We'll still be *smiling* when the evening comes!" The verse that he referred to says: "Whatever may pass, and whatever lies before me. Let me be *singing* when the evening comes." *("10,000 Reasons (Bless the Lord)," Matt Redman)* I still smile when I think of this monumental moment, a testimony of Todd's new-found confidence in God.

> **"Some trust in chariots and some in horses, but we trust in the name of the LORD our God."**
> **(Psalm 20:7, NIV)**

The next day Todd's eye pain partially subsided, but we now faced dealing with the weakness in the left side of his body. He was only slightly able to move his left arm and left leg. The rehabilitation team came to evaluate Todd and announced after the initial examination that with some intense therapy, Todd would eventually walk again. My heart sank for him. He faced four to six weeks of rehabilitative therapy.

After the rehab team left, Todd asked me if I had a song. Immediately, these words came to my mind: "Take my life and let it be all for You and for Your glory! Take my life and let it be Yours!" *("Glory to God Forever," Fee)* Todd had one, too, and began to sing, "There is power in the name of Jesus!" *("Break Every Chain," Tasha Cobbs)*

I prayed that evening for the Lord to help our family to shine, even in our darkest hours and trials of life. I realized again how short our lives really are and was reminded that this world is not our home. One day, every hurdle on earth will be a triumph in heaven, and I will say, "It was worth it ALL."

Todd moved from ICU to the neuro floor. As we awaited approval from our insurance company to receive inpatient rehab, realization dawned regarding the full scope of the abilities he had lost. This strong man had lost the ability to walk or even to stand on his own. My husband does not cry easily, but when I mentioned that his brothers offered to come and let me go home to gather some things, he broke down and cried. He feared he may never walk again. We embraced, cried together, and prayed. So much was coming at us, and it all seemed surreal.

After insurance approval, we moved to the Rehabilitation Unit on Monday, July 20, 2015. After Todd got settled and received his rigorous schedule of rehab, the doctors felt it might be a good idea for me to go back home while they worked with Todd for the first few days. He had a rough start due to his loss of independence and privacy, having to relearn how to dress and how to transfer himself safely from the bed to his wheelchair and from his wheelchair to a shower bench and back again. Next, he had the even more stressful and exhausting task of relearning to

133

balance and walk. He still had good leg strength, but he had lost the ability to freely move his left foot and had a dulled sense of feeling in his left foot and parts of his leg. He was fitted for a brace to keep his foot from rolling under him, and once he could see he was making progress, he worked tirelessly, determined to gain as much independence as possible.

Todd learned to walk short distances with the aid of his brace and three-point cane, and although it required a great deal of energy, he was happy to be able to get around without always being in a wheelchair. He developed severe spasmodic leg episodes during the night that robbed him of his sleep. The doctors tried several treatments from muscle relaxers to nerve medications, but they could not stop the spasms.

My husband's rehabilitation graduation was scheduled for Wednesday, August 5, 2015. I was excited but nervous at the same time. I had so many questions running through my mind. Would he be able to return to work? Would I be able to return to work? Would he be healed or would he get worse? Would we survive financially? I had to remind myself often that God was in control.

Graduation day arrived, and we were now free to leave the hospital on our own. By the grace of God, we made it safely home and by Saturday, Todd was surrounded with family who had eagerly awaited his return. It was so good to be back home. Todd was happy to see his yard, garden, and beloved garage. Our garage kitty, Sophie, seemed extra happy to see him, too.

After just a few days, we were scheduled for a follow up MRI and measles trial appointment. The MRI looked worse, but the doctor theorized that it was too early to know if it was inflammatory response due to the virus injection, which we wanted, or if it was actual tumor progression. Todd was not showing any increased or new deficits so he thought we should wait it out.

We finished our appointments early and went to use the restrooms before heading home. This made me nervous. Todd could ambulate haltingly, but he was at risk for falling. I had just walked out of the women's restroom and heard the men's electric door opening. As Todd exited the men's restroom, the door hit his shoulder, knocking him off balance, and he started to go down. I did what every good, Apostolic wife would do and yelled, "JESUS!" as I went lunging after him. As if I could catch him!

When I got to him, he said, "Why did you push me?" and started to laugh. As we both sat on the floor laughing, I told him laughing was not allowed because it made him wobbly. A gentleman, entering the restroom as I tried to assist Todd to a standing position, gave us a strange look and went back out. This, of course, only increased our laughter. Todd's ability to face his situation with some humor, even in the worst times, always impressed me.

136

Chapter Twenty-Five
Independent

Before getting discharged from the Rehab unit, we noticed some minor leakage from Todd's resection site. The doctors assured us that it did not appear infected but that we should keep an eye on it, and for safe measure, the neuro team only partially removed Todd's stitches and gave him a few more in the location of the drainage. They believed that radiation damage made the healing time longer, and we could have his stitches removed later in our hometown.

After returning home, Todd managed dressing, showering, and ambulating to use the bathroom on his own. He was still on sick leave with every intention of getting back to work.

He spent some time home alone, because he did not want us "babying him." I returned to work and even drove London back to IBC for her last year of college. While I was gone, my independent and stubborn husband gave himself heat stroke because he stayed out in his garage on one of the hottest days of summer. Our brave and resilient daughter, Ashton, once again came to his rescue in his time of need, even cleaning up his vomit because Todd could not move quickly enough to make it to the bathroom. The early morning phone call I received scared me half to death. When she first told me he was sick, my blood drained from my face, but then I asked if he was outside in his garage all day, and she said, "Yes."

I said, "I knew it!" I had warned him it was too hot to be out there.

Todd started his outpatient physical and occupational therapy sessions. He also scheduled an appointment to have his stitches removed by his family practitioner, but when he got to the appointment, the doctor was afraid to remove them because they had been in so long and looked difficult to remove. She sent him to see a plastic surgeon who removed them promptly, warning us the wound might open a little because it needed to heal from the bottom up. He instructed us to keep it dressed with ointment and to keep an eye on it.

Todd returned to work on August 24, 2015, and of course, he put in a full day! You just can't keep a good man down. He worked every day and came home exhausted in the evenings. I noticed that his wound seemed to have opened more than I thought it should, but I reasoned that I really knew nothing about wound healing. I called the plastic surgeon's nurse to ask her some questions, and she was somewhat curt with me and stated, "The doctor told you it would open some, and it has to finish healing from the bottom up. Does it look infected?"

I told her that it did not appear infected, but wondered if it could possibly be exposed bone. She again replied, "It's supposed to open up, and the doctor wasn't concerned about how it looked."

I hung up thinking, "Ok, maybe I'm wrong."

On Monday, August 31, 2015, Todd and I were getting ready for work, and as I helped him dress his wound, I saw a murky type of drainage. I called the plastic surgeon's office and asked if I could bring him in. As soon as the doctor saw the wound, he said, "Umm, that's his bone that you see. He needs wound cleaning and debridement, but I don't want to handle this here. I would like you to go back to Rochester and meet with your neuro-surgery team."

I thought, "Dear God, no! Not back to Rochester! Not another surgery!"

Both Todd and I returned to work, and I put a call into Todd's neuro-surgeon's office and spoke with his assistant, Lucinda, an amazing lady. When I told her the situation, she said, "We need him here as soon as possible." She told me to come directly to the emergency department, and she would alert the neurosurgery team and the plastic surgery team when we arrived. I booked two tickets out of Bismarck, and we were on our way back to Rochester that very evening.

140

Chapter Twenty-Six
We're Back!

We arrived back in Rochester late on Monday night and went to the emergency room early Tuesday morning. After check-in and the usual battery of questions, a neuro team member arrived to inform us that a plastic surgeon would come soon to analyze Todd's wound site and to get a culture to check for infection. To our relief, upon inspection of the wound, the neuro doctor stated that he did not believe the site looked infected.

When the plastic surgery doctor arrived, she agreed with the neuro doctor that the site did not look infected; however, she warned us that the cultures needed to sit a few days to make sure no strange bacteria grew before ruling out the possibility of infection. She also told us they would have to at least temporarily remove his bone flap, so Todd was checked in as an inpatient and scheduled for his plastic/neuro surgery procedure to close the incision.

The surgery team came and explained the procedure to us, predicting that if all went well, we could be out of the hospital by Friday or the following Monday. This news made us happy since we had already spent most of the summer in Rochester, and with fall soon approaching, we both just wanted to get back home as soon as possible.

For the first time since Todd's diagnosis, I felt like he should grant me power of attorney and possibly file for disability. I struggled to broach the subject, because I did not want to deflate his optimism or his faith in the Lord for complete healing.

Although I knew that God could heal and would if it was His will, I really felt in my spirit that I needed to get things signed over.

I love how the Lord, at the right time, just drops little things into our lives through His Word, through a song, or through a sensitive person who speaks encouragement. Our circumstances in life seemed to be changing at an accelerated rate, and one morning while driving in my car, I turned on the radio to a local Christian station. I rarely turn on the radio, choosing rather to drive in silence or play music from my phone, but the song that played that day was just for us:

There are days of taking more than I can give
And there are choices that I made that I wouldn't make again
I've had my share of laughter
Of tears and troubled times
This has been the story of my life

I have won
And I have lost
I got it right sometimes, but sometimes I did not
Life's been a journey
I've seen joy, I've seen regret
Oh, and You have been my God through all of it

You were there when it all came down on me
When I was blinded by my fear and I struggled to believe
But in those unclear moments You were the one keeping me strong
This is how my story's always gone

And this is who You are, more constant than the stars

Up in the sky, all these years, all my life
I, I look back and I see You
Right now I still do
And I'm always going to

("Through All of It," Colton Dixon)

September 4, 2015, they prepped my husband for surgery and took him away. This time I sat all alone, waiting for the outcome and praying all would go as planned. Reflecting over the events taking place, I thought back to my morning prayer time a year prior when the Lord warned me of a storm ahead. Then, to pass the time, I opened up my Pinterest feed, and as big as life, I saw this scripture: ***"When you pass through the waters, I will be with you…" (Isaiah 43:2, NIV)***

God reassured me that He is always in control, and I could trust Him. Not even one minute later, my co-worker and friend sent me a scripture picture she had found: ***Isaiah 43:2!***

After surgery, while Todd was in ICU for observation, he became very sick and nauseated, and only an hour after surgery an infectious disease doctor, completely covered in personal protective garments, entered the room. As I watched, they placed an infectious disease cart outside of Todd's hospital room door and hung signs outside of his room. The doctor explained that Todd's cultures did grow bacteria, and he had contracted an infectious disease called MRSA (Methicillin-resistant Staphylococcus aureus), which required a six-week, intravenous regimen of antibiotic treatments.

Early the next morning, Todd transferred across town to receive hyperbaric oxygen therapy to aid the healing of his wound. His pain was such that even the slightest movements made him ill, and the plastic surgeons told us that this intense pain was caused by the moving of muscles to get the skin to stretch over the wound site.

Todd was moved to a neurosurgical floor, and after two days, his pain was under control. He was also finally able to keep some fluids down. But, his relative inactivity exacerbated his left-sided weakness, causing swelling in his left hand and left foot. His left foot also felt hot to the touch, and when I showed this to the neurosurgeon, Dr. Parney, he immediately ordered an ultrasound and CAT scan.

On top of everything else, Todd now had developed a blood clot.

His doctor ordered a heparin drip to thin out his blood and a PICC line had to be inserted, because his IV site kept clogging. Dr. Parney ordered a new MRI before Todd's surgery, and although they saw new changes and more swelling, they had no clear answers regarding whether it was the injected virus at work or the progression of the disease.

However, even if the changes indicated disease progression, the neuro-oncologist said that all treatments would remain on hold due to the infection. We also knew that the remaining treatment options would only reduce symptoms, not result in a cure. We still needed a miracle!

Chapter Twenty-Seven
More Changes

After Todd's first full week in the hospital, I noticed changes that seemed unrelated to his wound and infection. He seemed to be losing interest in eating; he became very sleepy, and he was always looking to the right, even if I was talking to him from the left side. He wouldn't notice food on the left side of his food tray and would ask me what happened to his butter or coffee. No one seemed concerned at first, but with each passing day, he grew worse.

One morning, after observing Todd's behavior, Dr. Parney said he felt that brain swelling was causing most of the issues, so he decided to give him a bolus dose of Decadron, a steroid used in controlling brain swelling, to see if it would perk him up. He also told us we had a choice to make: hyperbaric oxygen therapy or inpatient rehab. We both knew Todd was losing ground with his mobility, and desperately wanting to get back home, Todd and I had a short discussion and chose rehab. The extra steroid perked Todd back up, but he still showed signs of left-sided neglect, as if he didn't know he had a left side to his body. It was very unnerving and sad.

While Todd rested, I slipped out to call his boss to let her know that Todd needed to file for disability. He was not the same person I had flown with to Rochester a week ago. I called his mother to let her know about the changes I saw, asking her to prepare his siblings, because without a divine healing, I feared we were losing him. It was one of the hardest phone calls I have ever made. Todd's mom, a neuro nurse for many years, knew exactly what I meant and remained strong and supportive. I said, "Please pray that we can get him well enough to come home. And, this is the last time we are returning to this place." We both agreed that if God didn't heal him, we were going to just love him and cherish every day we had left.

I hung up the phone, engulfed with sadness that I cannot explain. Unstoppable tears fell like rain, and as I sat there all alone in my corner, I felt a light touch, and a voice greeted me as "Sister Pace." When I looked up, I saw Pastor Kaske from the Pentecostals of Rochester, and moments later, a couple from the church that had been stopping in to pray for my husband during his last surgery also showed up. God sent them in my time of need.

I returned to Todd's hospital room, and we got him up in his wheelchair. After his extra strength shot of Decadron, he actually felt like eating supper, and in his more alert state, we began chatting when something came up about a rubber tree plant. My husband seemed to either have a song or make up a song for anything on a moment's notice, and he started to quote, "Just what makes that little old ant think he'll move that rubber tree plant? Anyone knows an ant can't...move a rubber tree plant."

I chuckled, "Where in the world did you get that from?"

Todd replied, "Haven't you ever heard that?"

"No, I don't believe I have," I answered.

He just couldn't believe that I had never heard it and stated, "You have to have! Everyone has! Look it up!"

So, I pulled out my iPad and looked it up. We found Frank Sinatra and began listening to him sing "High Hopes," while Todd sang along.

Next time you're found
With your chin on the ground.

There's a lot to be learned, so look around.
Just what makes that little old ant
Think he'll move that rubber tree plant.
Anyone knows an ant can't
Move a rubber tree plant
But he's got high hopes, he's got high hopes,
He's got high apple pie in the sky hopes.
So anytime you're gettin' low
'Stead of lettin' go,
Just remember that ant...
Oops, there goes another rubber tree plant!

("High Hopes," Frank Sinatra)

As he sang, tears rolled down both of our faces. He pointed at me, and as I looked at him, he exclaimed, "That's you!"

But, truthfully, the song was about him, a man of much strength and determination, always doing what others said he couldn't do. He had pushed through life many times, "But now, Jesus, his strength is gettin' low, and we need You to move our rubber tree plants!"

Our tears turned into laughter, and he quipped, "Once you hear it, you'll never forget it!"

He's right. I will never forget.

Chapter Twenty-Eight
Renewed Hope

One Tuesday morning, I retreated to my hotel room while Todd went to therapy. I felt defeated and needed a short prayer time before returning to meet my husband. Before entering the hospital doors, I stopped and read a plaque that had the hospital's motto with this scripture: *"And He healed them ALL!" (Matthew 12:15)* I felt a lift in my spirit and made up my mind to fast over the next three days. I said, "God, You ultimately get the final say, but the enemy cannot steal our HOPE (HIGH HOPE) or our JOY!"

I told Todd my plan, and he wanted to fast with me, but he already was not eating enough. I asked him to work on gaining his physical strength, just joining me in prayer, because I had the physical strength to fast, and the Lord would give both of us the spiritual strength that we needed.

I received numerous messages from people far and near that week that they were praying for us, or that God had put us on their hearts. I am ever grateful for the family of God.

Todd and I discussed our job situations. He talked to his boss on Saturday, September 12, 2015, because he remembered that was the day that his lab was to go live with their new electronic health records system. After he hung up, he shed tears, knowing I had applied for long-term disability for him. He also expressed thankfulness for how nice they had all been to him over the last few years, but mentioned that he was homesick for our children and grandkids. Thankfully, Ashton and

McKenzi were coming that very evening. Todd and I held many small prayer meetings to help get us through.

I was encouraged that morning by a devotion I was reading with these two scriptures:

"And so, after he had patiently endured, he obtained the promise." (Hebrews 6:15)

"Because you know that the testing of your faith produces perseverance." (James 1:3, NIV)

Chapter Twenty-Nine
Golden Dreams

I had completed my fast and was praying in my hotel in the evening before our daughters and granddaughter arrived. They pulled into town very late, and we all settled in for the night, planning to get up early and spend the morning at the hospital, then attend the evening church service.

That night I had a dream. I conversed with the Lord, but the details of our conversation are now very patchy. However, I do vividly remember that I looked up and saw this golden ball-like figure coming out of the sky, heading straight toward me. It moved at a moderate speed, leaving a golden trail behind as it descended. I remember just watching it, knowing it was going to land on me, but I did not move. I felt the ball hit the top of my head and heard it make an almost liquid-type "plop" sound that you would hear when a water balloon bursts open. I could feel it enter into my head. Immediately, I felt a strong presence of the Holy Ghost and started speaking in tongues. I woke up and realized I was speaking out loud, so I lay back down and fell asleep.

I feel like the dream had some meaning or significance for me. I don't know if it was the spiritual strength I told my husband the Lord would supply, if it was peace of mind, or if I will find out yet in the days ahead. One thing I knew for sure, God was near.

152

Chapter Thirty
Re-Entry of Rehab

On Monday, September 15, 2015, we received approval to move Todd back to inpatient rehabilitation, and although we were excited to get him strong enough to go home, we were depressed thinking about how much ground he had lost. His energy level and strength had decreased in just one short month, and he again developed some extremely painful and unexplainable, leg-jerking, muscle-spasm episodes that kept him awake at night. Several mornings, he scarcely had enough energy to make it to his physical therapy and occupational therapy sessions due to lack of sleep. However, this determined man persevered and made progress.

At one point during therapy, our children and grandchildren all stopped in for a few days to visit on their way to General Conference in Nashville, Tennessee. Todd and I listened online to some of the preaching of the conference, and Bro. Anthony Ens preached the message, "The Changing of Seasons," about how God is in control of the seasons that He allows in our lives.

Todd and I both understood, now more than ever, that we controlled nothing beyond our decision to put our trust in the Lord. After all, where else can a child of God go when He alone has the words of eternal life? Like Simon Peter asked, *"...Lord, to whom shall we go? You have the words of eternal life." (John 6:68, NIV)* Job also learned this lesson, for even in all of his suffering, he knew it would have been foolish to let go of God and not trust. He said, *"Though he slay me, yet will I trust in him..." (Job 13:15)* In spite of all we did not like or understand, we chose to put our trust in the Lord.

I called and talked to my friend and employer, Laurie, to let her know that I still did not know when I could return to work. I knew Todd would require constant care when we got home, and he became anxious when I was not with him. My life felt suspended in time, another month away from home and my family, and I had no definitive answers to give.

September 25, 2015 marked the 25th year of my own father's passing. At the age of twenty-three, I experienced the hard finality of losing a loved one, and now, twenty-five years later, I faced this possibility again, but this time, as a wife losing her husband. That evening, I listened to Bro. Bernard's conference message about "certifiable miracles" and prayed, "Jesus, Todd could be the next certified miracle! If You want to use his testimony to help us spread this message and give certified proof of Your power and Word, allow it in Jesus' Name!"

"The LORD thy God in the midst of thee is mighty..."
(Zephaniah 3:17)

Chapter Thirty-One
Homeward Bound

Todd was released from the rehabilitation unit on Monday, September 28, 2015. With just two short plane rides, we would be home with no plans of returning!

We struggled to get Todd on and off the plane, but the Lord helped us and we made it home. Todd's mom, his brother Scott, his sister Beth, and their spouses all welcomed us when we arrived, and Todd was so happy to see them and so happy to be home.

I now had the job of managing Todd's arsenal of antibiotics, administered through his PICC line, his Levanox injections for blood clots, his steroids for brain swelling, his seizure medications, and so on.

Todd was very restless and not sleeping well at night due to the continued leg spasms, so eventually I had to start sleeping on the couch. I also noticed he seemed unsteady while walking, a drastic regression from before, and once, in the middle of the night, he tried to get up out of bed and landed on the floor. Ashton and I somehow managed to get him off of the floor, but I mildly scolded him for not calling for help. He just couldn't accept his dependence on others. With my eyes, I could easily see that he did not have the same strength, steadiness, or endurance, but in his mind, he apparently thought he was doing just as well as before. Or, maybe it was just denial.

Due to his unsteady gait, I tried to stay close to his side whenever he walked with his cane, but he became frustrated with my hovering, so I had to refrain from being overprotective. I knew he needed my help, but I could not force him to accept it. He forced himself to get out of the house by refusing in-home patient therapy, opting for outpatient therapy instead. However, one day, on our way to do some errands, Todd lost his balance and fell in our driveway. I tried to help him up, but he no longer had the strength to assist me, so I could not lift him off the ground. Thankfully, the neighbor, our family friend, was able to come and help Todd up. He still wanted to do our errands, but I made him stay in his wheelchair rather than use his cane.

In addition to his declining balance and strength, one evening, Todd started feeling like he had a stiff neck and a headache-type feeling. I gave him some extra-strength Tylenol, and he slept for quite a while. While he rested, I prepared his favorite meal of cream chicken. He came out of his room to eat, but as soon as he finished, he asked to go back to bed. I got him settled, and he slept through the night.

At about 6:00 a.m. on Friday, October 2, 2015, he woke up, saying he needed to use the bathroom. He was weak and had a headache, so he agreed to use a urinal. I laid him back down, and immediately, he became nauseated and threw up but afterward managed to swallow a couple of Tylenol and fell asleep. I called his mom, explained his condition, and said, "I think he has extra brain swelling again," asking if his steroid level could be increased above the four milligrams a day he was currently taking. His mom talked to the doctor she worked with, the neurologist who assisted in Todd's care, and he increased the dose to twelve milligrams.

I prayed over Todd, believing that just one touch from Jesus would turn him around.

I also had a talk with Ashton, who still lived with us and was very helpful in caring for her dad, about the changes I observed. I explained that her dad was showing increased signs of end stages for this type of brain cancer. She broke down, not understanding why he had to go through all of this. I gently reminded her of God's mercy and of all the good things that had happened over the last two years. God, in His wisdom, had already extended Todd's life an extra twelve years when He healed him from stage IV lymphoma.

That same evening, I wrote down some thoughts on how I felt that God was using this time in our lives to mold and shape Todd, me, and our children if we would only allow the Potter's hand to shape us to be vessels of honor for Him.

I felt as if we were in a desert or wilderness-type place, a bit isolated from the rest of the world. Not because we didn't have others in our lives to help us, but more God showing me that there are some places in God that you must go alone. I thought of how the Lord had to agonize in the garden alone to carry the load of sin for all humanity. *"And he took them, and went aside privately into a desert place." (Luke 9:10)* I prayed, "Lord, help us to withstand any pressing that we feel or encounter along the way. Strengthen us!"

Todd stayed in bed the entire next day, complaining of horrible neck and shoulder pain. He also had moments of confusion, saying things that didn't make sense. For example, he wanted me to help him set up chairs one time or thought he saw flies another time.

His mother and siblings visited throughout that day, but he became so uncomfortable in our king-sized bed that his mother purchased him a lift chair so we could have his head propped up to relieve the pressure. His restlessness and confusion increased, and he did not eat or drink all day Friday and Saturday. By that evening, we knew his condition was worse, so McKenzi thought I should call London at college and let her know the situation. We arranged for her to come home the following Tuesday.

At about 11:00 p.m. on Saturday night, October 3, 2015, I pushed our king-size bed as close as I could beside Todd's lift chair and put my head on his shoulder. This seemed to calm him, and he went to sleep.

I woke up around 8:00 a.m. on Sunday, October 4, 2015, and while Todd slept, I showered and got ready for the day. At about 10:00 a.m., I peeked in the room to find him awake and fairly clear-headed, so I took my iPad into our room and we listened to our son-in-law preach the morning message. As he heard Andrew lead the congregation in prayer, he joined in with tears streaming down his face. After listening to the service, his mom arrived and was delighted to see him awake and alert. Todd asked me to get him into his wheelchair to take him out to the kitchen, because he wanted to eat again. It was looking like a good day.

On Monday morning, Todd woke up and had enough clarity to remember he had a doctor's appointment to remove his PICC line, since we had finally finished his antibiotic infusions for his MRSA infection.

Every day was unpredictable! One day he seemed better, and then the next day he would seem off. Sometimes he didn't sleep at night, starting to get something referred to as "Sundowners Syndrome" where he would think it was morning and want me to get up and make coffee. Other times, he remembered everything just as if nothing was wrong.

The life we once knew had disappeared; we lived more like shut-ins all of the time. I was unable to return to work, and Todd's health often prevented us from getting out to church service, which we both really missed. We were thankful for online communication.

I did not feel sorry for myself. I knew it was where I needed to be. I could not see what lay directly ahead from even one moment to the next.

During a morning devotion, I wrote down how everything in our life just seemed to stop: our daily routines, our jobs, our activities. I read a simple devotion that seemed to fit my situation and what I was thinking and feeling at that very moment. *"Who is among you that feareth the LORD, that obeyeth the voice of his servant, that walketh in darkness, and hath no light? let him trust in the name of the LORD, and stay upon his God." (Isaiah 50:10)*

I tried to read a Psalm and Proverb to my husband every day, and if he had the energy, we would read out of the Gospels. He was sensitive to God's Word and to songs of praise and would often weep as he would praise God or listen to His Word.

All of the bodily suffering and all of the neurological deficits that this disease brought never stole Todd's love for God.

At night, Todd could still not sleep due to leg and hip pain, so he resorted to dozing in his lift chair. I spent most of the night trying to shift his weight, fluffing pillows, or taking pillows away, but all my efforts only brought him brief moments of comfort.

I began noticing that the short distance he walked with his cane from our bedroom to the kitchen completely wiped him out. He still had the strong will to walk and move, but his body was saying, "No." One morning, he insisted on getting in the shower, rather than me helping him with a sponge bath, and by the time we finished, his body was perspiring from the effort of sitting on a shower bench. After helping him get dressed and back into his lift chair, I could tell he was sad, and he said, "That was way too hard!"

I did not know how to respond but finally said, "Daddy, I don't mind just giving you a sponge bath for now."

He replied, "You shouldn't have to work that hard."

I could tell he felt bad for me, but I assured him that he was not a burden to me. I thank God that He made a way for me to be there with my husband by providing for us financially through so many people's generous giving. I told him, "You would do no less for me," and I knew for certain that he would not have hesitated to take care of me if our roles had been reversed. I learned over the years that my husband loved me unconditionally.

Todd mustered up enough strength on Sunday, October 11, 2015, to attend our worship service at church where he worshipped with what little strength he had left. I could tell that all of the sights and sounds were over-stimulating his brain, because he kept staring off to the right. However, at the end of service, our daughters came to pray with us, and the Holy Ghost fell as Bro. Dale Jones from the Minnesota district prayed for our family and told my husband that he felt God was doing a great healing in our lives on many levels, not necessarily just physical. He felt God was going to use our family somehow, and Todd thanked him and said he believed God was doing great things as well.

Chapter Thirty-Two
Another Twist and Turn

Friday, October 16, 2015, Todd had a very restless and sleepless night; therefore, I did, too. I thought he was too tired to go get his stitches removed and to go to his occupational therapy session, but since we had cancelled a few already, he wanted to go.

As I observed him during the appointments, I did not like what I saw. He struggled to stay awake, and when I took him home, he could hardly eat the food I prepared for lunch without falling asleep. I got him comfortable in his lift chair and took the opportunity to shelter myself away with God.

Saturday dawned bright and sunny with the ground lightly kissed with frost, the sky clear and blue, and the air cool and crisp. I thought about the change of seasons. Soon, the colors of fall would give way to the white of winter and what the next season would bring, nobody knew.

I felt in my spirit that I was about to face another change, and I prayed, "Lord, please help me to be pliable. Help me to glean and learn from these life experiences to make me better and not bitter." I wanted God to help me look back and say, "God was ever at our side. Set us apart for Your glory."

"But God forbid that I should glory, save in the cross of our Lord Jesus Christ, by whom the world is crucified unto me, and I unto the world." (Galatians 6:14)

In the middle of that night, my husband experienced head and neck pain, and I could not get the pain under control with the little pain meds we had on hand. He begged me to help him and asked, "Is that all we can do?"

I prayed God would take the pain away or that the medications would be effective, but the pain was not subsiding. I finally knelt beside him, and with helpless tears streaming down my face, I pleaded, "Daddy, I need to call for help! I think we need to get hospice or home health involved." I knew he did not want to go back to the hospital, but we had reached the end of our options.

I called 911 to come and take Todd to our local emergency room and then called his mom to update her on the situation. She met us at the hospital, and after they got Todd's pain under control so he could sleep, she said, "Michelle, you need to get some help. You can't keep doing this on your own."

I knew she was right and told her how I had expressed this to Todd before we came to the hospital. I struggled, though, because I knew God was all-powerful! Did I have a lack of faith? Was I giving up?

The emergency room doctor admitted Todd to the hospital to allow us time to meet with hospice care and make arrangements at home for Todd's return.

That Sunday was a difficult day for our daughters as the reality of their dad's illness set in so vividly. Todd was only awake for brief periods of time, and his breathing patterns sounded agonal. Additionally, he kept hallucinating and talking confusedly.

During this hospital stay, we encountered heartaches mingled with tender moments of love and a renewed thankfulness for God's mercy toward us all.

I loved watching as our six-year old granddaughter, Nicollet, would lay her hands on her Papa and pray for his healing. One time in particular, she was sitting at my husband's bedside, watching over him, when she looked at me and said, "Should we pray for Papa again?" I agreed, so she laid her small hand on my husband, and my precious mother-in-law laid her hand on top of Nicollet's. Nicollet began to pray, asking that Jesus would take all of Papa's cancer and all of his pain and make him complete and whole in Jesus' Name!

He became more alert by late Monday afternoon, and as we visited, something came up about our three daughters. Todd got weepy and began to reach for Ashton. He wanted all of his girls, our son-in-law, and grandkids to come into his room. For about twenty minutes he held their hands and expressed to each one how he loved them. We all cried and prayed together. Never had we experienced such a real and tender moment together as a family.

On Tuesday, October 20, 2015, hospice arrangements were made and the hospice bed was sent to our home. The hospice doctor stopped in to visit with Todd while our friends from church, Wendlin and Roxanne Biegler, were visiting.

The doctor asked Todd about his brain tumor and how long he had been affected, and he was able to tell her how long. We mentioned to the doctor that God had spared Todd from much difficulty until this past summer in June when he started to show some loss of motor skills.

The doctor then asked my husband what he thought was the best thing that had happened over the last two years of his life. Without hesitation, Todd replied, "Receiving the Holy Ghost and building a relationship with Jesus."

She asked him more about what he believed, and he briefly gave her an account of his testimony. He told her there was nothing like having the Holy Ghost and knowing Jesus was always with you.

She then asked if he was afraid of what might happen in the future to which he replied, "No." He explained that he trusted that Jesus was going to take care of him no matter what.

When she inquired if he thought he would have come to know Jesus without having this disease, he looked at her and said, "No, I don't think I would have."

When she left, I said, "Dad! You just witnessed to her!"

He started to cry and said, "She needs to come to church." We gathered around Todd's bed and had a little prayer meeting for that doctor, and we thanked Him for the opportunity to be a witness for His holy name. It was a GOOD DAY!!

Chapter Thirty-Three
Home for Now

We brought Todd home on Wednesday afternoon, October 21, 2015.

London returned to Indiana to finish out the fall semester. She had mixed emotions about leaving but was thankful to have spent quality time and shared special moments with her dad. Todd was sad she had to go but told her she needed to go back and that it was ok.

I continued to struggle with the issue of Todd's healing. Our church had been in some great revival services with Bro. Robinette where God moved powerfully, and we were being covered in prayer in our home and out of our home by the saints in the church and by our pastor. I didn't think I lacked faith. But, did I?

On Friday, October 23, 2015, I prayed, "Lord, I do believe you can change this situation and heal Todd. You're my heavenly Father and You do not withhold good things from Your children. I don't feel like I have to beg for his healing. You have healed him before and You have saved him."

I felt God stop me, and He spoke to me, saying, "**Not all healing comes by giving breath in your lungs to continue on this earth. Healing comes from the inside, through My Spirit. Death, disease, and sickness have no power. These things will not keep him in the grave. My Spirit will raise him up on the last day. I have sealed him and healed him with the Holy Ghost of promise. What I have completed cannot be undone!**"

God confirmed the words that my friend, Sister Amanda, spoke to us months before in a church service before Todd's last tumor resection. I had peace that God was calling my husband to his real home.

These verses began to flood my mind:

"Where, O death, is your victory? Where, O death, is your sting? The sting of death is sin, and the power of sin is the law. But thanks be to God! He gives us the victory through our Lord Jesus Christ." (I Corinthians 15:55-57, NIV)

"For we know that if our earthly house of this tabernacle were dissolved, we have a building of God, an house not made with hands, eternal in the heavens." (II Corinthians 5:1)

Chapter Thirty-Four
The Unexpected

As the days passed, Todd seemed content to just stay in his room and rarely wanted to get out of bed. Even using the commode began causing difficulty for him as his legs weakened, causing him to cling to me or our daughter when transferring. One morning, after using the commode and struggling to stand and get back to bed, he apologized again for making me do all of this work for him. I reassured him that I would have it no other way.

My husband was not known for great patience, especially when faced with frustrating situations, and the working of the Holy Ghost in his life was so apparent. He treated us tenderly in the midst of great frustration and was more concerned about us than himself. Many times he would look at me and say, "You're so good to me."

He always wanted me very close by, and when people would come to visit and I would step out of the room, he would sometimes just call my name to see if I was still near.

One evening I asked Ashton if she would just stay with him while I ran to Target for a few things; I did not plan on being gone long. I told Todd where I was going and that I would be back soon. I had barely arrived at the store when my phone started ringing. Todd, upset and worried, wanted Ashton to get him in his wheelchair and into the car to come find me. I came home immediately and asked him, "Were you missing me?"

He said, "Yes, I don't know why I was like that," and he started to cry.

I reached over and prayed with him, knowing that this was all part of the effects on his brain from this disease.

On Friday, October 30, 2015, Todd's hospice nurse and a chaplain from the hospice program came out to honor Todd for being a veteran. They gave him a veteran pin and a few other keepsakes. We thanked them, and when they left, I settled in the recliner beside my husband.

At about three o'clock that afternoon, I received a text from my sister-in-law, Joy, asking if I knew where to find Todd's mom. I texted that she was not with us and that she should still be at work. A while later, Todd's mom called me and said, "Michelle, Bill was killed in a car accident today."

I couldn't believe what my ears were hearing. Bill was Todd's nephew from his oldest brother's family. With all that was happening, how could this be added to it? His car had rolled and he was gone. Todd understood when I told him, and we prayed for his brother, Scott, his sister-in law, Joy, and all of his siblings.

Todd was so concerned for Scott and his family. Even though getting out of the house was going to take an army, Todd insisted on getting out of his bed and attending Bill's funeral. He said, "I need to do what's right and be there for Scott, and I want to go out of respect for Bill." We accomplished the task of getting him to the funeral with much effort, and it was an emotional and exhausting day for all.

I continue to cover this family in prayer for healing, peace, and strength.

Chapter Thirty-Five
November

Todd was becoming confused more often, and his appetite was either very sporadic or fixated on only certain food items. He was still having some restless nights but seemed to be sleepier during the daytime hours.

On Sunday, November 8, 2015, I received a little snippet video of our youngest daughter singing for a benefit in Indiana. She sang the song "It is Well" by Bethel Music. As Todd listened to her sing, he started to pray quietly with tears rolling down his cheeks. The song was so fitting for everything that was taking place in our lives. It became a song I would often find myself singing in my head to get me through hard days.

That particular Sunday was one of the last times Todd ate anything substantial, which wasn't much. Although, he did express that carrot cake sounded good, so my friend, Jodi, and I whipped up some homemade carrot cake, which he ate.

By Tuesday, he was only taking small sips of liquid. I began putting Todd's pills into applesauce for him because it was becoming harder for him to swallow. He was fading before my eyes.

That evening, I settled myself in the recliner by Todd for the night, and as he drifted off to sleep, I noticed his breathing pattern sounded loud and labored. I listened for a while and tried to close my eyes, but I couldn't block it out and felt scared. I jumped out of my recliner, flipped on the lights and woke him up. I climbed into his hospital bed and lay down beside him with the lights on. We talked for a while until he drifted back to sleep. His breathing seemed to be less intense, so I went back to my chair and went to sleep.

On Wednesday evening, November 11, 2015, while Ashton was at church, Todd fell asleep and started breathing deep and heavy. I called Donna and Laurie, my dear friends, to come over and also called McKenzi to come out. I knew we were entering into the final days with Todd.

I called Pastor Gallion from Indiana Bible College and left a message that I needed to bring London back home for I feared Todd did not have much time left. Laurie made arrangements for London to come home the next evening.

On Thursday, November 12, 2015, I called Todd's mom to tell her what was going on. Todd was no longer accepting food outside of his tablespoon of applesauce. He was no longer drinking any liquids even when offered, and he was starting to sleep most of the time. I asked her to tell all of Todd's brothers and sisters about his condition and to let them know that they were welcome to be at our house as much as they needed or wanted to be. I called his hospice nurse to have her bring me liquid medications.

Todd's family started arriving that afternoon, and London arrived home that evening. Todd's mom and family helped me keep watch all night at Todd's bedside. They were sprawled out all over our house, even in the garage, and they never left our side. They were of great value and comfort to us.

Our bedroom became a sanctuary as we cared for Todd day and night. God's presence and peace were with us, and we filled his room with instrumental praises to God. We prayed with him, loved him, and cared for him.

Church family and friends served us. Our dear friend, Sara Woods, even gave up a few days of her life and stayed at my house and cleaned and cooked for Todd's family.

Several times Pastor Chuppe came to pray for Todd. On one visit in particular, we said, "Todd, Brother Chuppe is here."

Todd grinned and said, "That can't be good." He knew it meant he wasn't doing well.

It was a sorrowful time but also a time of drawing close to one another.

On Sunday, November 15, 2015, I texted Pastor Chuppe, and with one last-ditch effort of hope that God would change his mind and heal Todd, I said, "We need a NOW miracle!" Todd was changing again. He wasn't talking anymore. His only communication was to nod or say "ouch" when we moved him or cleaned him up. His morphine intake was now being given more frequently to control pain.

Our church family came that afternoon and stood outside of our bedroom window and prayed for Todd's miracle. I opened the windows so Todd could hear them. Pastor Chuppe and Brother Pete Magelky came inside and anointed Todd with oil.

That evening, Todd's baby sister, Brooke, had to return to Minot where she lived. She came into our bedroom to say her farewell.

I was not sleeping much and running on empty and had a few episodes of my own, screaming, "Jesus! Jesus!" in the middle of the night and causing everyone to scramble into our bedroom to find me sleeping again. One night, I fell to the floor from my bedside chair screaming out "Jesus!" as I proceeded to pass out on our bedroom floor. My poor, 75-year-old mother-in-law had her hands full. She ordered me to lie down on the recliner next to Todd; then, she ordered everyone else to go to bed as well. She, however, refused to lie down, and she and our nephew Tony stayed up with Todd while I rested.

Several nights, our daughters slept on our hard, laminate floor to be near their dad.

Night after night we thought he wouldn't make it through the night, and then he would pull through.

The Lord put a song in my heart during these days and it replayed in my head like a recording. I would find myself softly singing as I watched over Todd when we were in the room alone. The verse that I kept hearing is this:

I hear the voice.
The voice of the one I love
He's calling my name.
I hear the voice.
The voice of the one I love.
He's calling my name.
He's saying, Come up higher.
And hear the Angels sing
Come up higher my beloved.
Come up higher
And leave this world behind
I find you to be beautiful.

("Running," Gateway Worship)

I believe that Todd was hearing God calling him home, and the Lord used that song to bring me peace and comfort.

On Tuesday, November 17, 2015, at 9:00 in the evening, my faithful husband and friend went up higher and answered God's calling.

It was difficult to let him go. He was surrounded with his children, mother, most of his siblings, and a few nieces and a nephew.

Just before his final breath, I leaned over and whispered, "Daddy, I will see you later." This was not a forever goodbye!

The very next morning, I got a text from our niece telling me to look outside. I stepped outside my front door, and there, arcing almost right over our house, was a full rainbow! We live in North Dakota, and rainbows in wintery November are an extremely rare occurrence. But, God was reminding me that He had kept EVERY promise! It was well with my soul.

Chapter Thirty-Six
Running Down Below

Todd has been gone several months now. Our lives have been altered, but we have all been made richer in having loved and been loved by him.

I still hear his voice and his quirky jokes. I can close my eyes and see his grin.

I don't know what God has in store for me or for my children in the days and months ahead, but we must continue to walk by faith and not by sight.

I will now disclose the verse that stood out to me at that early Monday morning prayer time on September 15, 2014. I was reading my daily Proverb, and I felt this verse just leaped off of the page. We had just found out about Todd's first tumor recurrence at this time.

"The LORD tears down the house of the proud, but He makes secure the boundaries of the [consecrated] widow."
(Proverbs 15:25, AMP)

I was not sure at the time what to really think, but I wrote it down and now know that God gave me that verse. I can trust that the Lord will take care of me, and I can face my future without fear.

My prayer is to leave behind a legacy of grace for my children, their children, and the children to come if the Lord tarries.

"We will not hide them from their children, shewing to the generation to come the praises of the LORD, and his strength, and his wonderful works that he hath done." (Psalm 78:4)

Contact the Author

Thank you for taking the time to read my story. My deepest desire is that God would use this testimony to be a blessing in your life. If you would like to contact me, I can be reached via phone or email. May God bless you as your own legacy unfolds.

Phone: (701)390-9115
Email: michellepace1289@gmail.com